On Love

BY CHARLES BUKOWSKI

The Days Run Away Like Wild Horses Over the Hills (1969)

Post Office (1971)

Mockingbird Wish Me Luck (1972)

South of No North (1973)

Burning in Water, Drowning in Flame: Selected Poems 1955–1973 (1974)

Factotum (1975)

Love Is a Dog from Hell (1977)

Women (1978)

You Kissed Lilly (1978)

Play the Piano Drunk Like a Percussion Instrument Until the Fingers Begin to Bleed a Bit (1979)

Shakespeare Never Did This (1979)

Dangling in the Tournefortia (1981)

Ham on Rye (1982)

Bring Me Your Love (1983)

Hot Water Music (1983)

There's No Business (1984)

War All the Time: Poems 1981–1984 (1984)

You Get So Alone At Times That It Just Makes Sense (1986)

The Movie: "Barfly" (1987)

The Roominghouse Madrigals: Early Selected Poems 1946–1966 (1988)

Hollywood (1989)

Septuagenarian Stew: Stories & Poems (1990)

The Last Night of the Earth Poems (1992)

On Love

CHARLES BUKOWSKI

Edited by Abel Debritto

CANONGATE

Edinburgh · London

First published in Great Britain in 2016 by Canongate Books Ltd,
14 High Street, Edinburgh EH1 1TE

www.canongate.tv

1

Photograph on page 33 courtesy of Marina Bukowski.
All other photographs courtesy of Linda Lee Bukowski

First published in the USA by Ecco, an imprint of HarperCollins
Publishers, 195 Broadway, New York, NY, 10007

British Library Cataloguing-in-Publication Data
A catalogue record for this book is available on
request from the British Library

ISBN 978 1 78211 728 5

Printed and bound in Great Britain by Clays Ltd, St Ives plc.

MIX
Paper from
responsible sources
FSC® C020471

On Love

mine

She lays like a lump.
I can feel the great empty mountain
of her head
but she is alive. She yawns and
scratches her nose and
pulls up the covers.
Soon I will kiss her goodnight
and we will sleep.
And far away is Scotland
and under the ground the
gophers run.
I hear engines in the night
and through the sky a white
hand whirls:
goodnight, dear, goodnight.

layover

Making love in the sun, in the morning sun
in a hotel room
above the alley
where poor men poke for bottles;
making love in the sun
making love by a carpet redder than our blood,
making love while the boys sell headlines
and Cadillacs,
making love by a photograph of Paris
and an open pack of Chesterfields,
making love while other men—poor
fools—
work.

That moment—to this . . .
may be years in the way they measure,
but it's only one sentence back in my mind—
there are so many days
when living stops and pulls up and sits
and waits like a train on the rails.
I pass the hotel at 8
and at 5; there are cats in the alleys
and bottles and bums,
and I look up at the window and think,
I no longer know where you are,
and I walk on and wonder where
the living goes
when it stops.

the day I kicked a bankroll out the window

and, I said, you can take your rich aunts and uncles
and grandfathers and fathers
and all their lousy oil
and their seven lakes
and their wild turkey
and buffalo
and the whole state of Texas,
meaning, your crow-blasts
and your Saturday night boardwalks,
and your 2-bit library
and your crooked councilmen
and your pansy artists—
you can take all these
and your weekly newspaper
and your famous tornadoes
and your filthy floods
and all your yowling cats
and your subscription to *Life*,
and shove them, baby,
shove them.

I can handle a pick and ax again (I think)
and I can pick up
25 bucks for a 4-rounder (maybe);
sure, I'm 38
but a little dye can pinch the gray
out of my hair;
and I can still write a poem (sometimes),

don't forget *that*, and even if
they don't pay off,
it's better than waiting for death and oil,
and shooting wild turkey,
and waiting for the world
to begin.

all right, bum, she said,
get out.

what? I said.

get out. you've thrown your
last tantrum.
I'm tired of your damned tantrums:
you're always acting like a
character
in an O'Neill play.

but I'm different, baby,
I can't help
it.

you're different, all right!
God, how different!
don't slam
the door
when you leave.

but, baby, I *love* your
money!

4

you never once said
you loved me!

what do you want
a liar or a
lover?

you're neither! out, bum,
out!

. . . but baby!

go back to O'Neill!

I went to the door,
softly closed it and walked away,
thinking: all they want
is a wooden Indian
to say yes and no
and stand over the fire and

not raise too much hell;
but you're getting to be
an old man, kiddo:
next time play it closer
to the
vest.

I taste the ashes of your death

the blossoms shake
sudden water
down my sleeve,
sudden water
cool and clean
as snow—
as the stem-sharp
swords
go in
against your breast
and the sweet wild
rocks
leap over
and
lock us in.

love is a piece of paper torn to bits

all the beer was poisoned and the capt. went down
and the mate and the cook
and we had nobody to grab sail
and the N.wester ripped the sheets like toenails
and we pitched like crazy
the bull tearing its sides
and all the time in the corner
some punk had a drunken slut (my wife)
and was pumping away
like nothing was happening
and the cat kept looking at me
and crawling in the pantry
amongst the clanking dishes
with flowers and vines painted on them
until I couldn't stand it anymore
and took the thing
and heaved it
over
the side.

to the whore who took my poems

some say we should keep personal remorse from the
poem,
stay abstract, and there is some reason in this,
but jezus:
12 poems gone and I don't keep carbons and you have
my
paintings too, my best ones; it's stifling:
are you trying to crush me out like the rest of them?
why didn't you take my money? they usually do
from the sleeping drunken pants sick in the corner.

next time take my left arm or a fifty
but not my poems:
I'm not Shakespeare
but sometimes simply
there won't be any more, abstract or otherwise;
there'll always be money and whores and drunkards
down to the last bomb,
but as God said,
crossing his legs,
I see where I have made plenty of poets
but not so very much
poetry.

shoes

shoes in the closet like Easter lilies,
my shoes alone right now,
and other shoes with other shoes
like dogs walking avenues,
and smoke alone is not enough
and I got a letter from a woman in a hospital,
love, she says, love,
more poems,
but I do not write,
I do not understand myself,
she sends me photographs of the hospital
taken from the air,
but I remember her on other nights,
not dying,
shoes with spikes like daggers
sitting next to mine,
how these strong nights
can lie to the hills,
how these nights become quite finally
my shoes in the closet
flown by overcoats and awkward shirts,
and I look into the hole the door leaves
and the walls, and I do not
write.

a real thing, a good woman

they are always writing about the bulls, the bullfighters,
those who have never seen them,
and as I break the webs of the spiders reaching for my wine
the umhum of bombers, gd.dmn hum breaking the solace,
and I must write a letter to my priest about some 3rd. st. whore
who keeps calling me up at 3 in the morning;
up the old stairs, ass full of splinters,
thinking of pocket-book poets and the priest,
and I'm over the typewriter like a washing machine,
and look look the bulls are still dying
and they are razing them raising them
like wheat in the fields,
and the sun's black as ink, black ink that is,
and my wife says Brock, for Christ's sake,
the typewriter all night,
how can I sleep? and I crawl into bed and
kiss her hair sorry sorry sorry
sometimes I get excited I don't know why
friend of mine said he was going to write about
Manolete . . .
who's that? nobody, kid, somebody dead
like Chopin or our old mailman or a dog,
go to sleep, go to sleep,
and I kiss her and rub her head,
a good woman,
and soon she sleeps and I wait
for morning.

one night stand

the latest hardware dangling upon my pillow catches
window lamplight through the mist of alcohol.

I was the whelp of a prude who whipped me when
the wind shook blades of grass the eye could see
move and
you were a
convent girl watching the nuns shake loose
the Las Cruces sand from God's robes.

you are
yesterday's
bouquet so sadly
raided. I kiss your poor
breasts as my hands reach for love
in this cheap Hollywood apartment smelling of
bread and gas and misery.

we move through remembered routes
the same old steps smooth with hundreds of
feet, 50 loves, 20 years.
and we are granted a very small summer, and
then it's
winter again
and you are moving across the floor
some heavy awkward thing

and the toilet flushes, a dog barks
a car door slams . . .
it's gotten inescapably away, everything,
it seems, and I light a cigarette and
await the oldest curse
of all.

the mischief of expiration

I am, at best, the delicate thought of a delicate hand
that quenches for the mixing rope, and when
beneath the love of flowers I am still,
as the spider drinks the greening hour—
strike gray bells of drinking,
let a frog say
      a voice is dead,
let the beasts from the pantry
and the days that have hated this,
the contrary wives of unblinking grief,
plains of small surrender
between Mexicali and Tampa;
hens gone, cigarettes smoked, loaves sliced,
and lest this be taken for wry sorrow:
put the spider in wine,
tap the thin skull sides that held poor lightning,
make it less than a treacherous kiss,
put me down for dancing
you much more dead,
I am a dish for your ashes,
I am a fist for your air.

the most immense thing about beauty
is finding it gone.

love is a form of selfishness

pither, the eustachian tube and the green bugdead ivy
and the way we walked tonight
with the sky climbing on our ears and in our pockets
while we talked of things that didn't matter
and the streetcar rocked and howled its color
which we didn't notice except as a thing beside the eve
as we mentioned sex through palsies,
pither, the red fire, pither the eustachian tube!
gone are the days, gone is the green bugdead ivy
and the words we said tonight that didn't matter;
X 12, Cardinal and Gold
            GOLD GOLD GOLD GOLD GOLD!
your eyes are gold
        your hair is gold
            your love is gold
                your grave is gold
and the streets go past like people walking
and the bells ring like bells ringing;
your hands are gold and your voice is gold
and all the children walking
and the trees growing and the idiots selling papers
34256780000 oh while you are

eustachian tube
    red fire
        greenbugdead
           ivy
cardinal and gold
and the words we said tonight
are going away
           over the trees
down by the streetcar
and I have closed the book
       with the red red lion
down by the gates of gold.

*for Jane: with all the love I had, which was
not enough*

I pick up the skirt,
I pick up the sparkling beads
in black,
this thing that moved once
around flesh,
and I call God a liar,
I say anything that moved
like that
or knew
my name
could never die
in the common verity of dying,
and I pick
up her lovely
dress,
all her loveliness gone,
and I speak
to all the gods,
Jewish gods, Christ-gods,
chips of blinking things,
idols, pills, bread,
fathoms, risks,
knowledgeable surrender,
rats in the gravy of 2 gone quite mad

without a chance,
hummingbird knowledge, hummingbird chance,
I lean upon this,
I lean on all of this
and I know:
her dress upon my arm:
but
they will not
give her back to me.

for Jane

225 days under grass
and you know more than I.

they have long taken your blood,
you are a dry stick in a basket.

is this how it works?

in this room
the hours of love
still make shadows.

when you left
you took almost
everything.

I kneel in the nights
before tigers
that will not let me be.

what you were
will not happen again.

the tigers have found me
and I do not care.

Charles Bukowski
1623 N. Mariposa Ave.
Los Angeles, 27, Calif.

FOR JANE: WITH ALL THE LOVE I HAD,
WHICH WAS NOT ENOUGH:--

I pick up the skirt,
I pick up the sparkling beads
in black,
this thing that moved once
around flesh,
and I call God a liar,
I say anything that moved
like that
or knew
my name
could ever die
in the common verity of dying,
and I pick
up her lovely
dress,
all her lovliness gone,
and I speak
to all the gods,
Jewish gods, Christ-gods,
chips of blinking things,
idols, pills, bread,
fathoms, risks,
knowledgeable surrender,
rats in the gravy of 2 gone quite mad
without a chance,
hummingbird knowledge, hummingbird chance,
I lean upon this,
I lean on all of this:
and I know:
her dress upon my arm:
but
they will not
give her back to me.

notice

the swans drown in bilge water,
take down the signs,
test the poisons,
barricade the cow
from the bull,
the peony from the sun,
take the lavender kisses from my night,
put the symphonies out on the streets
like beggars,
get the nails ready,
flog the backs of the saints,
stun frogs and mice for the cat of the soul,
burn the enthralling paintings,
piss on the dawn,
my love
is dead.

my real love in Athens

and I remember the knife,
the way you touch a rose
and come away with blood
and how you touch love the same way,
and how when you want to come onto the freeway
the trucks rail you on the inner lane
moonlight and roaring
running down your bravery,
making you touch the brakes
and small pictures come to your mind:
pictures of Christ hung there
or Hiroshima,
or your last wife
frying an egg.

the way you touch a rose
is the way you lean against the coffin-sides
of the dead,
the way you touch a rose
and see the dead whirling back
underneath your fingernails;
the knife
Gettysburg, the Bulge, Flanders,
Attila, Muss—

what can I make of history
when it narrows down
to the three o'clock shadow
under a leaf?

and if the mind grows harrowed
and the rose bites
like a dog,
they say
we have love . . .

but what can I make of love
when we are all born
at a different time and place
and only meet
through a trick of centuries
and a chance three steps
to the left?

you mean
a love I have not met
is less than a selfishness
I call near?

can I say now
with rose-blood upon the edge of mind,
can I say now as the planets whirl
and they shoot tons of force into the end of space
to make Columbus look like an idiot-child,
can I say now

that because I have screamed into a night
and they have not heard,
can I say now
that I remember the knife
and I sit in a cool room
and rub my fingers to the whistle of the clock
and calmly think of
Ajax and sputum
and railroad hens across the golden rails,
and my real love is in Athens
600
A or B,
as outside my window
pigeons stumble as they fly
and through a door
that outwaits an empty room,
roses can't get
in or out,
or love or moths or lightning—
I would neither break upon sighing
or smile; could nothings
like moths and men
exist like orange sunlight upon paper
divided by nine?

Athens is now many miles
and one death away,
and the tables are dirty as hell
and the sheets and the dishes,
but I'm laughing: that's not real;

but it is, divided by nine
or one hundred:
clean laundry is love
that does not scratch itself
and sigh.

sleeping woman

I sit up in bed at night and listen to you
snore
I met you in a bus station
and now I wonder at your back
sick white and stained with
children's freckles
as the lamp divests the unsolvable
sorrow of the world
upon your sleep.

I cannot see your feet
but I must guess that they are
most charming feet.

who do you belong to?
are you real?
I think of flowers, animals, birds
they all seem more than good
and so clearly
real.

yet you cannot help being a
woman. we are each selected to be
something. the spider, the cook.
the elephant. it is as if we were each

a painting and hung on some
gallery wall.

—and now the painting turns
upon its back, and over a curving elbow
I can see ½ a mouth, one eye and
almost a nose.
the rest of you is hidden
out of sight
but I know that you are a
contemporary, a modern living
work
perhaps not immortal
but we have
loved.

please continue to
snore.

a party here—machineguns, tanks, an army
fighting against men on rooftops

if love could go on like tarpaper
or even as far as meaning goes
but it won't work
can't work
there are too many snot-heads
too many women who hide their legs
except for special bedrooms
there are too many flies on the
ceiling and it's been a hot
Summer
and the riots in Los Angeles
have been over for a week
and they burned buildings and killed policemen and
                                        whitemen and
I am a whiteman and I guess I did not get particularly
excited because I am a whiteman and I am poor
and I pay for being poor
because I do as few handstands for somebody else as
                                        possible
and so I'm poor because I *choose* it and I guess it's
not as uncomfortable that
way

and so I ignored the riots
because I figured both the black and the white
wanted many things that did not interest
me
plus having a woman here who gets very excited about
discrimination the Bomb segregation
you know you know
I let her go on until finally the talk
wearies me
for I don't care too much for the
standard answer
or the lonely addled creatures who like to join a
CAUSE simply because a cause lifts them out of their

                                              dribbling

imbecility into a stream of
action. me, I like time to think, think, think . . .
but it was a party here, really, machineguns, tanks,
the army fighting against men on rooftops . . .
the same thing we accused Russia of doing. well, it's
a lousy game, and I don't know what to do, except
if it's like a friend of mine said I said one night when
I was drunk: "Don't ever kill anybody, even if it seems
like the last or the only thing to do."
laugh. all right. it might make you happy
that I even have a stream of remorse when I kill a
fly. an ant. a flea. yet I go on. I kill them and
go on.

    god, love is more strange than numerals more strange
                                        than
grass on fire more strange than the dead body of a child

drowned in the bottom of a tub, we know so
little, we know so much, we don't know
enough.

     anyhow, we go through our movements, bowel,
                                 sometimes
sexual, sometimes heavenly, sometimes bastardly, or
sometimes we walk through a museum to see what is
left of us or it, the sad strictured palsy of glassed
and frozen and sterile madhouse background
enough to make you want to walk out into the sun again
and look around, but in the park and on the streets
the dead keep on moving through as if they were already
in a museum. maybe love is sex. maybe love is a bowl of
mush. maybe love is a radio shut off.

anyway, it was a party.
a week ago.

today I went to the track with roses in my eyes. dollars in
                                    my
pocket. headlines in the alley. it's over a hundred miles by
                                   train,
one way. a party of drunks coming back, broke again, the
                                 dream
shot again, bodies wobbling; yakking in the barcar and I'm
                             in there
too, drinking, scribbling what's left of hope in the dim light,
                                 the
barman was a Negro and I was white. bad fix. we made
it.

no party.

the rich newspapers keep talking about "The Negro
                                    Revolution" and
"The Breakdown of the Negro Family." the train hit town,
                                    finally,
and I got rid of the 2 homosexuals who were buying me
                                    drinks, and I
went to piss and make a phonecall and as I came through
                                    the
entranceway to the Men's crapper here were 2 Negroes at a
                                    shoeshine
stand shining the shoes of whitemen and the whitemen let
                                    them do
it.

        I walked down to a Mexican bar
and had a few whiskeys and when I left the barmaid gave
                                    me a
little slip of paper with her name, address and phone
                                    number upon
it, and when I got outside   I threw it into the gutter
got into my car and drove   down into Western Los
                                    Angeles
and everything looked the same   the same as it always
                                    did
and at Alvarado and Sunset I   slowed to 40
I saw a policeman   fat on his cycle
looking prompt and heinous
and I was disgusted with myself and

everyone, all the little any of us
had done, love, love, love,
and the towers swayed like old stripteasers
praying for the lost magic, and I drove on in
shining the shoes of every Negro and Gringo in
America, including
my own.

for the 18 months of Marina Louise

sun sun
is my little
girl
sun
on the carpet—
sun sun
out the
door
picking a
flower
waiting for me
to rise
and
play.

an old man
emerges
from his
chair,
battle-wrecked,
and she looks
and only
sees
love, which I

become
through her
majesty
and infinite
magic
sun.

poem for my daughter

(they tell me that I am now a
responsible citizen, and through sun stuck on Northern
windows of dust
red camellias are flowers crying while
babies are crying.)

I spoon it
in: strained chicken noodle dinner
junior prunes
junior fruit dessert

spoon it in and
for Christ's sake
don't blame the
child
don't blame the
govt.
don't blame the bosses or the
working classes—

spoon it down
through these arms and chest
like electrocuted
wax

a friend phones:
"Whatya gonna do now, Hank?"
"What the hell ya mean, what am I gonna
do?"
"I mean ya got responsibility, ya gotta bring the
kid up
right."

feed her:
spoon it
down:
a place in Beverly Hills
and never any need for unemployment compensation
and never to sell to the highest
bidder

never to fall in love with a soldier or a killer of any
kind

to appreciate Beethoven and Jellyroll Morton and
bargain dresses

she's got a
chance:
there was once the
Theoric Fund and now there's the
Great Society

"Are ya still gonna play the horses? are ya still gonna
drink? are ya still gonna—"

"yes."

telephone, waving flower in the wind & the dead bones of
my heart—
now she sleeps beautifully like
boats on the Nile

maybe some day she will
bury me

that would be very nice

if it weren't a
responsibility.

answer to a note found in the mailbox

"love is like a bell
tell me, have you
heard it in her voice?"

love is not like a bell
that's poetic, true,
but I've heard something in her voice
that in the puke of my misery
that in death's head sitting in the window
grinning its broken yellow teeth
has risen me to a climate I have seldom
known—
"here, a flower. I bring flower."
I hear something in her voice
that has nothing to do with sweating and tricky and
bleeding armies
that has nothing to do with the factory boss with broken
eyes

I am not picking at your words:
you have your bell
I have this and maybe you have this
too:
"I bring shoes. shoe. shoe. here is
shoe!"

it is more than learning what a shoe is
it is more than learning what I am or what she
is
it is something else
that maybe we who have lived a long time have almost
forgotten

that a child should come from the swamps of my pain
bearing flowers, actually bearing flowers,
christ, this is almost too much
that I should be allowed to see with eyes and touch and
laugh,
this knowledgeable beast of me
frowns inside
but soon finds the effort too much to hide
behind
and this small creature who knows me so well
crawls all through and over me
Lazarus Lazarus
and I am not ashamed
warrior slammed through by hours and years of
waste
love is like a bell
love is like a purple mountain
love is like a glass of vinegar
love is all the graves
love is a train window
she knows my name.

all the love of me goes out to her (for A.M.)

cleverly armed with arguments to the Pope
I make my way among the non-electric people
to seek reasons for my death and my living;
it is a charming day for those who like the days—
for those who wait upon the night
as I do, then day is shit and shit is for
sewers,
and I open the door of a tiny cafe
and a waitress in dark blue
walks up as if I had ordered *her.*
"3 pheasants legs," I tell her,
"the back of a chicken and 2 bottles of fair French
wine."
she leaves
twitching in her blue
and all the love of me goes out to her
but there is no way,
and I sit looking at the plants
and I say to the plants, with my mind,
can't you love me?
can't something happen here?
must the sidewalks always be sidewalks, must the generals
continue to laugh in their dreams,
must it always continue to be
that nothing is true?

I look to my left and see a man picking his nose;
he slides the residue under a
chair; quite true, I think, there's your
truth, and there's your love:
snot hardening under a chair during
hot nights when hell comes up and simply
spits all over
you.
plants, I say, can't you?
and I break off part of an elephant leaf
and the whole ceiling splits apart
heaven is a stairway down,
the waitress walks up and says,
"will that be all, sir?"
and I say, "yes, thank you, that is
enough."

an answer to a critic of sorts

a lady will perhaps meet a man
because of the way he writes
and soon the lady might be suggesting
another way of writing.

but if the man loves the lady
he will continue to write the way he does
and if the man loves the poem
he will continue to write the way he must

and if the man loves the lady and the poem
he knows what love is
twice as much as any other man

I know what love is.
this poem is to tell the lady that.

the shower

we like to shower afterwards
(I like the water hotter than she)
and her face is always soft and peaceful
and she'll wash me first
spread the soap over my balls
lift the balls
squeeze them,
then wash the cock:
"hey, this thing is still hard!"
then get all the hair down there—
the belly, the back, the neck, the legs,
I grin grin grin,
and then I wash her . . .
first the cunt, I
stand behind her, my cock in the cheeks of her ass
I gently soap up the cunt hairs,
wash there with a soothing motion,
I linger perhaps longer than necessary,
then I get the backs of the legs, the ass,
the back, the neck, I turn her, kiss her,
soap up the breasts, get them and the belly, the neck,
the fronts of the legs, the ankles, the feet,
and then the cunt, once more, for luck . . .
another kiss, and she gets out first,

toweling, sometimes singing while I stay in
turn the water on hotter
feeling the good times of love's miracle
I then get out . . .
it is usually mid-afternoon and quiet,
and getting dressed we talk about what else
there might be to do,
but being together solves most of it,
in fact, solves all of it
for as long as those things stay solved
in the history of woman and
man, it's different for each
better and worse for each—
for me, it's splendid enough to remember
past the marching of armies
and the horses that walk the streets outside
past the memories of pain and defeat and unhappiness:
Linda, you brought it to me,
when you take it away
do it slowly and easily
make it as if I were dying in my sleep instead of in
my life, amen.

2 carnations

my love brought me 2 carnations
my love brought me red
my love brought me her
my love told me not to worry
my love told me not to die

my love is 2 carnations on a table
while listening to Schoenberg
on an evening darkening into night

my love is young
the carnations burn in the dark;
she is gone leaving the taste of almonds
her body tastes like almonds

2 carnations burning red
as she sits far away
now dreaming of china dogs
tinkling through her fingers

my love is ten thousand carnations burning
my love is a hummingbird sitting that quiet moment
on the bough
as the same cat
crouches.

have you ever kissed a panther?

this woman thinks she's a panther
and sometimes when we are making love
she'll snarl and spit
and her hair comes down
and she looks out from the strands
and shows me her fangs
but I kiss her anyhow and continue to love.
have you ever kissed a panther?
have you ever seen a female panther enjoying
the act of love?
you haven't loved, friend.
you with your little dyed blondes
you with your squirrels and chipmunks
and elephants and sheep.
you ought to sleep with a panther
you'll never again want
squirrels, chipmunks, elephants, sheep, fox,
wolverines,
never anything but the female panther
the female panther walking across the room
the female panther walking across your soul;
all other love songs are lies
when that black smooth fur moves against you
and the sky falls down against your back,

the female panther is the dream arrived real
and there's no going back
or wanting to—
the fur up against you,
the search is over
as your cock moves against the edge of Nirvana
and you are locked against the eyes of a panther.

the best love poem I can write at the moment

listen, I told her,
why don't you stick your tongue
up my
ass?

no, she said.

well, I said, if I stick my tongue
up your ass first
then will you stick your tongue
up my
ass?

all right, she said.

I got my head down there
and looked around,
I opened a section,
then moved my tongue forward . . .

not there, she said,
o, hahaha, not there, that's not
the right place!

you women have more holes than
swiss cheese . . .

I don't want you
to do
it.

why?

well, then I'll have to do it
back and then at the next party
you'll tell people I licked your ass
with my tongue.

suppose I promise not to
tell?

you'll get drunk, you'll
tell.

o.k., I said, roll over,
I'll stick it in the
other place.

she rolled over and I stuck my tongue
in that other place.

we were in love

we were in love
except with what I said at
parties

and we were not in love
with each other's
assholes.

she wants me to write a love poem
but I think if people
can't love each other's
assholes

and farts and shits and terrible parts
just like they love
the good parts,
that ain't complete love.

so as far as love poems go
as far as we have gone,
this poem will have to
do.

THAT'S WHAT YOU GET
FOR YOUR SEXISM.

balling

balling
balling like the mule
balling like the ox
balling balling balling
balling like the pigeons
balling like the pigs

how does one become a flower
pollinated by the winds and the bees?

balling at midnight
balling at 4 a.m.
balling on Tuesday
balling on Wednesday
balling like a bleeding bull
balling like a submarine
balling like a taffy bar
balling like the senseless cavity of doom
balling balling balling,
I plunge my white whip in
feeling her eyes roll in glory,
o balls, o trumpet and balls
o white whip and balls, o
balls,

I could go on forever balling
on top
on bottom
sideways
drunk sober sad happy angry
balling,
an intensity of admixture:
2 souls stuck together
spurting . . .
balling makes everything better.
those who do not ball do not know.
those who cannot ball are half-dead.
those who cannot find somebody to ball are in hell.
I sleep with my balls in my hand so nobody will steal them.

may the entire air be clean with flowers and trees and bulls.
may some of the justice of our living be the song of the body.
may each of our deaths and half-deaths be as easy as
                                                    possible now.
meanwhile, o balls, o balls, o bells, o balls of bells, bells
of balls, o balls balling balls o balling balls of mine and
yours and theirs and them and ours forever and the day
tonight and Tuesday Wednesday of the crying grave, I love
                                        you
ladies, I love you.

hot

she was hot, she was so hot
I didn't want anybody else to have her,
and if I didn't get home on time
she'd be gone, and I couldn't bear that—
I'd go mad . . .
it was foolish I know, childish,
but I was caught in it, I was caught.

I delivered all the mail
and then Henderson put me on the night pickup run
in an old army truck,
the damn thing began to heat halfway through the run
and the night went on
me thinking about my hot Miriam
and jumping in and out of the truck
filling mailsacks
the engine continuing to heat up
the temperature needle was at the top
HOT HOT
like Miriam.

I leaped in and out
3 more pickups and into the station
I'd be, my car

waiting to get me to Miriam who sat on my blue couch
with scotch on the rocks
crossing her legs and swinging her ankles
like she did,
2 more stops . . .
the truck stalled at a traffic light, it was hell
kicking it over
again . . .
I had to be home by 8, 8 was the deadline for Miriam.

I made the last pickup and the truck stalled at a signal
½ block from the station . . .
it wouldn't start, it couldn't start . . .
I locked the doors, pulled the key and ran down to the
station . . .
I threw the keys down . . . signed out . . .
"your god damned truck is stalled at the signal,
Pico and Western . . ."

. . . I ran down the hall, put the key into the door,
opened it . . . her drinking glass was there, and a note:

> *sun of a bitch:*
>> *I wated until 5 after ate*
>> *you don't love me*
>> *you sun of a bitch*
>> *somebody will love me*
>> *I been wateing all day*
>>> *Miriam*

I poured a drink and let the water run into the tub
there were 5,000 bars in town
and I'd make 25 of them
looking for Miriam

her purple teddy bear held the note
as he leaned against a pillow

I gave the bear a drink, myself a drink
and got into the hot
water.

smiling, shining, singing

my daughter looked like a very young Katharine Hepburn
at the grammar school Christmas presentation.
she stood there with them
smiling, shining, singing
in the long dress I had bought for her.

she looks like Katharine Hepburn, I told her mother
who sat on my left.
she looks like Katharine Hepburn, I told my girlfriend
who sat on my right.
my daughter's grandmother was another seat away;
I didn't tell her anything.

I never did like Katharine Hepburn's acting,
but I liked the way she looked,
class, you know,
somebody you could talk to in bed
with an hour and a half before going to
sleep.

I can see that my daughter is going to be a most
beautiful woman.
someday when I get old enough
she'll probably bring me the bedpan with a most
kindly smile.

and she'll probably marry a truckdriver with a very
heavy walk
who bowls every Thursday night
with the boys.
well, all that doesn't matter.
what matters is now.

her grandmother is a great hawk of a woman.
her mother is a psychotic liberal and lover of life.
her father is a drunk.

my daughter looked like a very young Katharine Hepburn.
after the Christmas presentation
we went to McDonald's and ate, and fed the sparrows.
Christmas was a week away.
we were less worried about that than nine-tenths of the town.
that's class, we both have class.
to ignore life at the proper time takes a special wisdom:
like a Happy New Year to
you all.

visit to Venice

we took a walk along the shore at Venice
the hippies sitting waiting on Nirvana
some of them flogging bongos,
the last of the old Jewish ladies waiting to die
waiting to follow their husbands so long gone,
the sea rolled in and out,
we got tired and stretched out on some lawn
and my 8 year old daughter ran her fingers through
my beard, saying, "Hank, it's getting whiter and
whiter!" I laughed straight up into the sky, she was
so funny. then she touched my mustache, "It's getting
white too." I laughed again. "How about my eyebrows?"
I asked. "There's one there. It's half white and half
red."
"yeah?" "yes."
I closed my eyes a moment. she ran her fingers through my
hair. "But there's no white in your hair, Hank. Not one
hair is white . . ."
"No, here by the right ear," I said, "it's starting."
we got up and continued our walk to the car.
"Frances has all white hair," she said.
"Yes," I said, "but it's those 5 long white hairs that
hang from her chin that don't look too well."
"Is that why you left each other?"

"No, she claimed I went to bed with another woman."

"Did you?"

"Look how high the sky is!"

the sea rolled in and out.

"She won't get any men to kiss her with those 5 white hairs
on her chin."

"But she does!"

"Oh yeah?"

"Well, not too many . . ."

"50,000?"

"Oh, no . . ."

"5?"

"Yes, 5. One man for each hair."

we got back into the car and I drove her back to
her mother.

love poem to Marina

my girl is 8
and that's old enough to know
better or worse or
anything
so I relax around her and
hear various astounding things
about sex
life in general and life in particular;
mostly it's very
easy
except I became a father when most men
become grandfathers, I am a very late starter
in everything,
and I stretch on the grass and sand
and she rips dandelions up
and places them in my
hair
while I doze in the sea breeze.
I awaken
shake
say, "what the hell?"
and flowers fall over my eyes and over my nose
and over my lips.

I brush them away
and she sits above me
giggling.

daughter,
right or wrong,
I do love you,
it's only that sometimes I act as if
you weren't there,
but there have been fights with women
notes left on dressers
factory jobs
flat tires in Compton at 3 a.m.,
all those things that keep people from
knowing each other and
worse than
that.

thanks for the
flowers.

I can hear the sound of human lives being ripped to pieces

strange warmth, hot and cold females,
I make good love, but love isn't just
sex, and most females I've known are
very ambitious, and I like to lie around
on large pillows on mattresses at 3 o'clock
in the afternoon, I like to watch the sun
through the leaves of a bush outside
while the world out there
holds away from me, I know it so well, all
those dirty pages, and I like to lie around
my belly up to the ceiling after making love
everything flowing in:
nectarines, used boxing gloves, history books of the
Crimean War;
it's so easy to be easy—if you like it, that's all
that's necessary.
but the female is strange, she is very
ambitious—"Shit! I can't sleep away the day!
Eat! Make love! Sleep! Eat! Make love!"

"My dear," I tell her, "there are men out there now
picking tomatoes, lettuce, even cotton,
there are men and women dying under the sun,

there are men and women dying in factories
for nothing, a pittance . . .
I can hear the sound of human lives being ripped to
pieces . . .
you don't know how lucky we
are . . ."

"But you've got it made," she says,
"your poems . . ."

my love gets out of bed.
I hear her in the other room.
the typewriter is working.

I don't know why people think effort and energy
have anything to do with
creation.

I suppose that in matters like politics, medicine,
history and religion
they have been lied to
also.

I turn on my belly and fall asleep with my
ass to the ceiling.

for those 3

going crazy
sitting around listening to Chopin
waltzes, having slept with 3 different women
in 3 different states
in two weeks, the pace has been
difficult, sitting in airport bars
holding hands with beautiful ladies
who had read Tolstoy, Turgenev and
Bukowski.
amazing how completely a lady can give her
love—when she wants
to.
now the ladies are far away
and I sit here barefooted
unshaven, drinking beer and
listening to these Chopin
waltzes, and
thinking of each of the ladies
and I wonder if they think of me
or am I just a book of poems
lost in with other books of poems?
lost in with Turgenev and Tolstoy.
no matter. they gave enough.
when they touch my book now
they will know the shape of my body
they will know my laughter and my love and
my sadness.
my thanks.

blue moon, oh bleweeww mooooon
how I adore you!

I care for you, darling, I love you,
the only reason I fucked L. is because you fucked
Z. and then I fucked R. and you fucked N.
and because you fucked N. I had to fuck
Y. But I think of you constantly, I feel you
here in my belly like a baby, love I'd call it,
no matter what happens I'd call it love, and so
you fucked C. and then before I could move again
you fucked W., so then I had to fuck D. But
I want you to know that I love you, I think of you
constantly, I don't think I've ever loved anybody
like I love you.

bow wow bow wow wow
bow wow bow wow wow.

the first love

at one time
when I was 14
the creators brought me
my only feeling of
chance.

my father disliked
books and
my mother disliked
books (because my father
disliked books)
especially those I brought back
from the library:
D. H. Lawrence
Dostoyevsky
Turgenev
Gorky
A. Huxley
Sinclair Lewis
others.

I had my own bedroom
but at 8 p.m.

we were all supposed to go to sleep:
"Early to bed and early to rise
makes a man healthy, wealthy and wise,"
my father would say.

"LIGHTS OUT!" he would shout.

then I would take the bed lamp
place it under the covers
and with the heat and the hidden light
I would continue to read:
Ibsen
Shakespeare
Chekov
Jeffers
Thurber
Conrad Aiken
others.

they brought me chance and hope and
feeling in a place of no chance
no hope, no feeling.

I worked for it.
it got hot under the covers.
sometimes the lamp would begin to smoke
or the sheets—there would be a
burning;
then I'd switch the lamp off,
hold it outside to
cool off.

without those books
I'm not quite sure
how I would have turned
out:
raving; the
murderer of the father;
idiocy; imbecility;
drab hopelessness.

when my father shouted
"LIGHTS OUT!"
I'm sure he feared
the well-written word
that appeared with gentleness
and reasonableness
in our best and
most interesting
literature.

and it was there
close to me
under the covers
more woman than woman
more man than man.

I had it all
and
I took it.

love

Sally was a sloppy
leaver. she was good with the
notes,
she wrote them with a large
indignant hand, she was
good at that.

and she always took most of her
clothes,
but I'd open the bottle
sit down and look about—
and there'd be a pink slipper
under the bed.
I'd finish the drink
and get down under the bed
to get that pink slipper and
throw it in the trash
and next to the pink slipper
I'd find a pair of shit-stained
panties.

and there were hairpins everywhere:
in the ashtray, on the dresser, in the
bathroom. and her magazines were
everywhere with their exotic covers:

"Man Rapes Girl, Then Throws Her Body from
400 Foot Cliff."
"9 Year Old Boy Rapes 4 Women in Greyhound
Bus-Stop Restroom, Sets Fire to Repository
Disposal Units."

Sally was a sloppy leaver.
in the top drawer next to the Kleenex
I'd find all the notes I'd ever written her,
neatly bound with 3 or 4 sets of rubber
bands.

and she was sloppy with
photos:
I'd find one of both of us
crouched on the hood of our
'58 Plymouth—
Sally showing a lot of leg
and grinning like a Kansas City gun-moll
from out of the
twenties,
and me
showing the bottoms of my shoes
with the circular waving holes
in them.

and, there were photos of dogs,
all of them ours,
and, photos of children,
most of them
hers.

every hour and twenty minutes
the phone would ring
and it would be
Sally
and a song from the juke
box, some song I
hated, and she'd keep talking
and I'd hear men's
voices:

"Sally, Sally, forget the fuckin' phone,
come on and sit down back,
baby!"

"you see," she'd say, "there are other men in the
world besides you."
"your opinion only," I'd answer.
"I could have loved you forever, Bandini," she'd say.
"get fucked," I'd say and hang
up.

Bandini is manure all right
but it was also the name I had given myself
after a rather emotional and rather childish character
in a novel written by some
Italian in the 1930s.

I'd pour another drink
and while looking for a scissors in the bathroom
to trim the hair around my ears
I'd find a brassiere in one of the drawers

and hold it up to the light.
the brassiere looked all right from the outside
but inside—there was this stain of
sweat and dirt, and the stain was darkened,
molded in there
as if no washing would ever
take it
out.

I'd drink my drink
then begin to trim the hair around my ears
deciding that I was quite a handsome man.
but I'd lift the weights
go on a diet
get a tan,
anyhow.

then the phone would ring again
and I'd lift the receiver
hang up
lift the receiver again
and let it
dangle
by the cord.

I'd trim my ear hairs, my nose, my
eyebrows,
drink another hour or two,
then go to
sleep.

I'd be awakened by a sound I had never quite
heard before—
it felt and sounded like a warning of
atomic attack.
I'd get up and look for the sound.
it would be the telephone
still off the hook
but the sound that came from it
was much like a thousand wasps
burning to death. I'd
pick up the
phone.

"sir, this is the desk clerk. your phone is
off the hook."

"all right sorry. I'll
hang up."

"don't hang up, sir. your wife is on the
elevator."

"my wife?"

"she says she's Mrs. Budinski . . ."

"all right, it's
possible . . ."

"sir, can you get her off the
elevator? she doesn't understand the
controls . . . her language is abusive toward us

but she says that you'll
help her . . . and, sir . . ."

"yes? . . ."

"we didn't want to call the
police . . ."

"good . . ."

"she's lying down on the floor on the
elevator, sir, and, and . . . she has . . .
urinated upon
herself . . ."

"o.k.," I'd say and
hang up.

I'd walk out in my shorts
drink in hand
cigar in mouth
and press the elevator
button.
up it would come:
one, two, three, four . . .
the doors would open
and there would be
Sally . . . and little delicate
trickles and ripples of water lines
drifting about the elevator
floor, and some blotchy
pools.

I'd finish the drink
pick her up and
carry her out of the
elevator.

I'd get her to the apartment
throw her on the bed
and pull off her wet
panties, skirt and stockings.
then I'd put a drink on the coffee table
near her
sit down on the couch
and have another for
myself.

suddenly she'd sit straight up and
look around the
room.

"Bandini?" she'd ask.
"over here," I'd
wave my hand.

"o, thank god . . ."

then she'd see the drink and
drink it right
down. I'd get up,
refill it, put cigarettes, ashtray and
matches
nearby.

then she'd sit up again:
"who took my panties
 off?"

"me."

"me, who?"

"Bandini . . ."

"Bandini? you can't
 fuck me . . ."

"you pissed
 yourself . . ."

"who?"

"you . . ."

 she'd sit straight
 upright:
"Bandini, you dance like a
 queer, you dance like a
 woman!"

"I'll break your god damned
 nose!"

"you broke my arm, Bandini, don't you go
 breaking my nose . . ."

then she'd put her head back on the
pillow: "I love you, Bandini, I really
do . . ."

then she'd start snoring. I'd drink another
hour or two then
I'd get into bed with
her. I wouldn't want to touch her
at first. she needed a bath, at
least. I'd get one leg up against hers;
it didn't seem too
bad. I'd try the
other.
I'd start to remember all the good days and the
good nights . . .
slip one arm under her neck,
then I'd have the other around her
belly and my drunken penis
gently up against her
crotch.

her hair would come back
and climb into my nostrils.
I'd feel her inhale heavily, then
exhale. we'd sleep like that
most of the night and into the
next afternoon. then I'd get up and
go to the bathroom and vomit
and then she'd
have her turn.

raw with love (for N.W.)

little dark girl of
kindness
when it comes time to
put the knife
I won't blame
you.
and when I drive down the shore
and the palms wave,
the ugly heavy palms
and the living do not arrive
and the dead do not leave,
I won't blame you.
I will remember the hours of kisses
our lips raw with love
and how you offered me
your cunt your soul your insides
and how I answered
offering you whatever was left of
me,
and I will remember the shape of your room
the shape of you
your records
your walls
your coffee cups
your mornings and your noons and your nights

and your toilet and your
bathtub.
our bodies spilled together
sleeping
these tiny flowing currents
immediate and forever
crossing
criss-crossing
again and again.
your leg my leg
your arm my arm
your sadness and loss and warmth
also mine,
I have memorized you
each shape of you
the feel of your cunt-hairs in my teeth
gently-pulling, and
you
who made me laugh at the
appropriate times
always.
little dark girl of kindness
you have no
knife. it's
mine and I don't want to use it
yet.

THEN LOVE CAME.

a love poem for all the women I have known

all the women
all their kisses the
different ways they love and
talk and need.

their ears they all have
ears and
throats and dresses
and shoes and
automobiles and ex-
husbands.

mostly
the women are very
warm they remind me of
buttered toast with the butter
melted
in.

there is a look in the
eye: they have been
taken they have been
fooled. I don't know quite what to
do for
them.

I am
a fair cook a good
listener
but I never learned to
dance—I was busy
then with larger things.

but I've enjoyed their different
beds
smoking cigarettes
staring at the
ceilings. I was neither vicious nor
unfair. only
a student.

I know they all have these
feet and barefoot they go across the floor as
I watch their bashful buttocks in the
dark. I know that they like me, some even
love me
but I love very
few.

some give me oranges and pills;
others talk quietly of
childhood and fathers and
landscapes; some are almost
crazy but none of them are without
meaning; some love
well, others not
so; the best at sex are not always the

best in other
ways; each has limits as I have
limits and we learn
each other
quickly.

all the women all the
women all the
bedrooms
the rugs the
photos the
curtains, it's
something like a church only
at times there's
laughter.

those ears those
arms those
elbows those eyes
looking the fondness and
the waiting I have been
held I have been
held.

fax

it beats love because
there aren't any wounds
flopping about. in the
morning she turns on the
radio to Brahms or Ives
or Stravinsky or Mozart.
she boils the eggs count-
ing the seconds out loud:
56, 57, 58. she peels
the eggs, brings them to
me in bed. after break-
fast it's the couch, we
put our feet on the same
chair and listen to the
classical music. she's
on her first glass of
scotch and her third
cigarette. I tell her
I must go to the race-
track. she's been about
2 nights and 2 days.
"when will I see you
again?" I ask. she suggests
that might be up to me.
I nod and Mozart plays.

one for the shoeshine man

the balance is in the snails climbing the
Santa Monica cliffs;
the luck is in walking down Western Avenue
and having one of the girls from a massage
parlor holler at you, "Hello, Sweetie!"
the miracle is in having five women in love
with you at the age of 55,
and the goodness is that you are only able
to love one of them.
the gift is in having a daughter more gentle
than you are, whose laughter is finer
than yours.
the placidity is in being able to drive a
blue 67 Volks through the streets like a
teenager, the radio on to The Host Who Loves You
Most, feeling the sun, feeling the solid hum
of the rebuilt motor
as you needle through traffic
pissing-off the dead.
the grace is in being able to like rock music,
symphony music, jazz . . .
anything that contains the joy of original
energy.

and the mathematic that returns
is the deep blue low
yourself flat upon yourself
within the guillotine walls—
angry at the sound of the phone
or anybody's footsteps passing;
and the other mathematic:
the imminent lilting high that follows
making the guys who sit on the benches
outside the taco stands
look like gurus
making the girl at the checkstand in the
supermarket look like
Marilyn
like Zsa Zsa
like Jackie before they got her Harvard lover
like the girl in high school that
all us boys followed home.

and the neatness which makes you believe
in something else besides death
is Sandy Hawley bringing in
five winners at Hollywood Park on off-form horses,
none of them favorites,
or somebody in a car approaching you
on a street too narrow,
and he or she pulls aside to let you
by, or the old fighter Beau Jack
shining shoes
after blowing the entire bankroll
on parties
on women

on parasites,
humming, blowing on the leather,
working the rag,
looking up and saying:
"What the hell, I had it for a
while. that beats the
other."

I act very bitter sometimes
but the taste has often been
sweet, it's only that I've
feared to say it. it's like
when your woman says,
"tell me you love me," and
you can't say it.

if you ever see me grinning from
my blue Volks
running a yellow light
driving straight into the sun
without dark shades
I will only be locked into the
afternoon of a
crazy life
thinking of trapeze artists
of midgets with big cigars
of a Russian winter in the early forties
of Chopin with his bag of Polish soil
or an old waitress bringing me an extra
cup of coffee and seeming to laugh at me
as she does so.

the best of you
I like more than you think.
the others don't count
except that they have fingers and heads
and some of them eyes
and most of them legs
and all of them
good and bad dreams
and a way to go.

the balance is everywhere and it's working
and the machineguns and the frogs
and the hedges will tell you
so.

who in the hell is Tom Jones?

I was shacked
with a 24 year old
girl from New York
City for two weeks,
along about the time
of the garbage strike
out there, and one night
this 34 year old woman
arrived and she said,
"I want to see my rival,"
and she did and then
she said, "o, you're a
cute little thing!"
next I knew there was a
whirling of wildcats—
such screaming and scratching,
wounded animal moans,
blood and piss . . .

I was drunk and in my
shorts. I tried to
separate them and fell,
wrenched my knee. then
they were through the

door and down the walk
and out in the street.

squadcars full of cops
arrived. a police helicopter
circled overhead.

I stood in the bathroom
and grinned in the mirror.
it's not often at the
age of 55
that such splendid
action occurs.
it was better than the
Watts riots.

then the 34 year old
came back in. she had pissed
all over herself and her
clothing was torn and
she was followed by 2 cops
who wanted to know
why.

pulling up my shorts
I tried to explain.

sitting in a sandwich joint just off the freeway

my daughter is most
glorious.
we are eating in my
car in Santa Monica.
I say, "Hey, kid,
my life has been
good, so good."
she looks at me.
I put my head down
lean over the steering
wheel, then I kick
the door open, "I'm a
GENIUS!"
then I put on a mock-
puke.
she laughs, biting
into her sandwich.
I straighten up,
pick up 4 french fries,
put them into my mouth,
chew them.
it is 5:30 p.m.
and the cars run up
and down past
us.

I sneak a look.
she's grinning,
her eyes bright with
the remainder of the
world.
we've got all the luck
we need.

a definition

love is nothing but headlights at
night running through the fog

love is nothing but a beercap
that you step on while on the way
to the bathroom

love is a lost key to your door
when you're drunk

love is what happens one day a
year
one year in ten

love is the crushed cats
of the universe

love is an old newsboy on the
corner who has
given it up

love is the first 3 rows of
potential killers at the
Olympic Auditorium

love is what you think the other
person has destroyed

love is what vanished with the
age of battleships

love is the phone ringing
and the same voice or another
voice but never the right
voice

love is betrayal
love is the burning of the
wino in the alley

love is steel
love is the cockroach
love is a mailbox

love is rain upon the roof
of the cheapest hotel
in Los Angeles

love is your father in a coffin
who hated you

love is a horse with the
broken leg
trying to stand on it
while 55,000 people
watch

love is the way we boil
like the lobster

love is a filter cigarette
stuck in your mouth and
lighted the wrong way

love is everything we said
it wasn't

love is the Hunchback of
Notre Dame

love is the flea you can't
find

love is the mosquito

love is 50 grenadiers

love is the emptier of
bedpans

love is a riot at Quentin
love is a madhouse full
love is a donkey shitting in a
street of flies

love is a barstool when there is
nobody sitting on it

love is a film of the Hindenburg
curling to pieces
in years that still scream

love is Dostoyevsky at the
roulette wheel

love is what crawls along
the ground

love is your woman dancing
pressed against a stranger

love is an old woman
pinching a loaf of bread

love is a word used
constantly
ever most constantly

love is red roofs and green
roofs and blue roofs
and flying in jet airliners

that's all.

an acceptance slip

16 years old
during the Depression
I'd come home drunk
and all my clothing—
shorts, shirts, stockings,
suitcase, and pages of
short stories
would be thrown on the
front lawn and about the
street.

my mother would be waiting
behind a tree:
"Henry, Henry, don't
go in . . . he'll
kill you, he's read
your stories . . ."

"I can whip his
ass . . ."

"Henry, please take
this . . . and
find yourself a room."

but it worried him
that I might not
finish high school
so I'd be back
again.

one evening he walked in
with the pages of
one of my short stories
(which I had never submitted
to him)
and he said, "this is
a great short story,"
and I said, "o.k.,"
and he handed it to me
and I read it.
it was a story about
a rich man
who had a fight with
his wife and had
gone out into the night
for a cup of coffee
and had noticed
the waitress and the spoons
and forks and the
salt and pepper shakers
and the neon sign
in the window
and then had gone back
to his stable
to see and touch his

favorite horse
who then
kicked him in the head
and killed him.

somehow
the story held
meaning for him
though
when I had written it
I had no idea
of what I was
writing about.

so I told him,
"o.k., old man, you can
have it."

and he took it
and walked out
and closed the door.
I guess that's
as close
as we ever got.

the end of a short affair

I tried it standing up
this time.
it usually doesn't
work
this time it seemed
to be . . .

she kept saying,
"oh my god, you've got
beautiful legs!"

it was all right
until she took her feet off the
ground
and wrapped her legs
around my center.

"oh my god, you've got
beautiful legs!"

she weighed about 138
pounds and hung there as I
worked.

it was when I climaxed
that I felt the pain
fly straight up my
spine.

I dropped her on the
couch and walked around
the room.
the pain remained.

"look," I told her,
"you'd better go. I've got
to develop some film
in my dark room."

she dressed and left
and I walked into the
kitchen for a glass of
water. I got a glass full
in my left hand.
the pain ran up behind my
ears and
I dropped the glass
which broke on the floor.

I got into a tub full of
hot water and Epsom salts.
I just got stretched out
when the phone rang.
as I tried to straighten
my back
the pain extended to my
neck and arms.
I flopped about,
gripped the sides of the tub,
got out
with shots of green and yellow

and red light
whirling in my head.

the phone kept ringing.
I picked it up.
"hello?"

"I LOVE YOU!" she said.

"thanks," I said.

"is that all you've got
to say?"

"yes."

"eat shit!" she said and
hung up.

love dries up, I thought
as I walked back to the
bathroom, about as fast as
sperm.

"IT'S NOT WORKING, IS IT?" BUK

one for old snaggle-tooth

I know a woman
who keeps buying puzzles
Chinese
puzzles
blocks
wires
pieces that finally fit
into some order.
she works it out
mathematically
she solves all her
puzzles
lives down by the sea
puts sugar out for the ants
and believes
ultimately
in a better world.
her hair is white
she seldom combs it
her teeth are snaggled
and she wears loose shapeless
coveralls over a body most
women would wish they had.
for many years she irritated me

with what I considered her
eccentricities—
like soaking eggshells in water
(to feed the plants so that
they'd get calcium).
but finally when I think of her
life
and compare it to other lives
more dazzling, original
and beautiful
I realize that she has hurt fewer
people than anybody I know
(and by hurt I simply mean hurt).
she has had some terrible times,
times when maybe I should have
helped her more
for she is the mother of my only
child
and we were once great lovers,
but she has come through
like I said
she has hurt fewer people than
anybody I know,
and if you look at it like that,
well,
she has created a better world.
she has won.

Frances, this poem is for
you.

prayer for a whore in bad weather

by God, I don't know what to
do.
they're so nice to have around.
they have a way of playing with
the balls
and looking at the cock very
seriously
twisting it
tweaking it
examining each portion
as their long hair drops along
your belly.

it's not the fucking and sucking
alone
that reaches into a man
and softens him,
it's the extras,
it's all the extras.

now it's raining tonight
and there's nobody about.
they are elsewhere
examining things

in new bedrooms
in new moods
or maybe in old
bedrooms.

anyhow, it's raining tonight,
one hell of a dashing, pouring
rain . . .
very little to do.
I've read the newspaper
paid the gas bill
the electric co.
the phone bill.

it keeps raining.

they soften a man
and then let him swim
in his own juices.

I need an old-fashioned whore
at the door tonight
folding her green umbrella,
drops of moonlit rain on her
purse, saying, "shit, man,
you can get better music
than *that* on your radio . . .
and turn up the heat . . ."

it's always when a man's
horny with love and everything
else

that it just keeps raining
splattering
vomiting
rain
good for the trees and the
grass and the air . . .
good for things that can
live alone.

I would give anything
for a female's hand on my balls
tonight.
they get to a man and
then leave him listening
to the rain.

I HAVEN'T HAD A PIECE
OF ASS IN FOUR YEARS.

I made a mistake

I reached up into the top of the closet
and took out a pair of blue panties
and showed them to her and
asked "are these yours?"

and she looked and said,
"no, those belong to a dog."

she left after that and I haven't seen
her since. she's not at her place.
I keep going there, leaving notes stuck
into the door. I go back and the notes
are still there. I take the Maltese cross
cut it down from my car mirror, tie it
to her doorknob with a shoelace, leave
a book of poems.
when I go back the next night everything
is still there.

I keep searching the streets for that
blood-wine battleship she drives
with a weak battery, and the doors
hanging from broken hinges.

I drive around the streets
an inch away from weeping,
ashamed of my sentimentality and
possible love.

a confused old man driving in the rain
wondering where the good luck
went.

the 6 foot goddess (for S.D.)

I'm big
I suppose that's why my women have seemed
small
but this 6 foot goddess
who deals in real estate
and art
and flies from Texas
to see me
and I fly to Texas
to see her—
well, there's plenty of her to
grab hold of
and I grab hold of it
of her,
I yank her head back by the hair,
I'm real macho,
I suck on her upper lip
her cunt
her soul
I mount her and tell her,
"I'm going to shoot some white hot
juice into you. I didn't fly all the

way to Galveston to play
chess."

later we lay locked like human vines
my left arm under her pillow
my right arm over her side
I grip both of her hands,
and my chest
belly
balls
cock
tangle into her
and through us in the dark
pass white whooping rays
back and forth
back and forth
until I fall away
and we sleep.

she's wild
but kind
my 6 foot goddess
makes me laugh
the laughter of the mutilated
who still need
love,
and her blessed eyes
run deep into her head
like inward fountains
far in

and
cool and good.

she has saved me
from everything that is
not here.

I BEGAN TO SUCK THE AIR OUT OF HER LUNGS.

quiet clean girls in gingham dresses

all I've ever known are whores, ex-prostitutes,
madwomen. I see men with quiet,
gentle women—I see them in the supermarkets,
I see them walking down the streets together,
I see them in their apartments: people at
peace, living together. I know that their
peace is only partial, but there is
peace, often hours and days of peace.

all I've ever known are pill freaks, alcoholics,
whores, ex-prostitutes, madwomen.

when one leaves
another arrives
worse than her predecessor.

I see so many men with quiet clean girls in
gingham dresses
girls with faces that are not wolverine or
predatory.

"don't ever bring a whore around," I tell my
few friends, "I'll fall in love with her."

"you couldn't stand a good woman, Bukowski."

I need a good woman. I need a good woman
more than I need this typewriter, more than
I need my automobile, more than I need
Mozart; I need a good woman so badly that I
can taste her in the air, I can feel her
at my fingertips, I can see sidewalks built
for her feet to walk upon,
I can see pillows for her head,
I can feel my waiting laughter of easy joy,
I can see her petting a cat,
I can see her sleeping,
I can see her slippers on the floor.

I know that she exists
but where is she upon this earth
as the whores keep finding me?

I JUST WAKE UP IN TIME.

tonight

"your poems about the girls will still be around
50 years from now when the girls are gone,"
my editor phones me.

dear editor:
the girls appear to be gone
already.

I know what you mean

but give me one truly alive woman
tonight
walking across the floor toward me

and you can have all the poems

the good ones
the bad ones
or any that I might write
after this one.

I know what you mean.

do you know what I mean?

pacific telephone

you go for these wenches, she said,
you go for these whores,
I'll bore you.

I don't want to be shit on anymore,
I said,
relax.

when I drink, she said, it hurts my
bladder, it burns.

I'll do the drinking, I said.

you're waiting for the phone to ring,
she said,
you keep looking at the phone.
if one of those wenches phones you'll
run right out of here.

I can't promise you anything, I said.

then—just like that—the phone rang.

this is Madge, said the phone. I've
got to see you right away.

oh, I said.

I'm in a jam, she continued, I need ten
bucks—fast.

I'll be right over, I said, and
hung up.

she looked at me. it was a wench,
she said, your whole face lit up.
what the hell's the matter with
you?

listen, I said, I've got to leave.
you stay here. I'll be right back.

I'm going, she said. I love you but you're
crazy, you're doomed.

she got her purse and slammed the door.

it's probably some deeply-rooted childhood fuckup
that makes me vulnerable, I thought.

then I left my place and got into my Volks.
I drove north up Western with the radio on.
there were whores walking up and down
both sides of the street and Madge looked
more vicious than any of them.

hunchback

moments of damnation and moments of glory
tick across my roof.

the cat walks by
seeming to know everything.

my luck has been better, I think,
than the luck of the gladiola,
although I am not sure.

I have been loved by many women,
and for a hunchback of life,
that's lucky.

so many fingers through my hair
so many hands grasping my balls
so many shoes tilted sideways across my bedroom
rug.

so many eyes looking,
indented into a skull that will carry all those
eyes into death,
remembering.

I have been treated better than I should have
been—
not by life in general
or the machinery of things
but by women.

and the other
(by women): me
standing in the bedroom alone
doubled
hands holding the gut—
thinking
why why why why why why?

women gone to men like pigs
women gone to men with hands like dead branches
women gone to men who fuck badly
women gone to things of men
women gone
gone
because they must go
in the order of
things.

the women know
but more often chose out of
disorder and confusion.

they can kill what they touch.
I am dying
but not dead.

mermaid

I had to come into the bathroom for something
and I knocked
and you were in the tub
you had washed your face and your hair
and I saw your upper body
and except for the breasts
you looked like a girl of 5, of 8
you were gently gleeful in the water
Linda Lee.
you were not only the essence of that
moment
but of all my moments
up to there
you bathing easily in the ivory
yet there was nothing
I could tell you.

I got what I wanted in the bathroom
something
and I left.

yes

no matter who I'm with
people always say,
are you still with her?

my average relationship lasts
two and one half years.
with wars
inflation
unemployment
alcoholism
gambling
and my own degenerate nervousness
I think I do well enough.

I like reading the Sunday papers in bed.
I like orange ribbons tied around the cat's neck.
I like sleeping up against a body that I know well.

I like black slips at the foot of my bed
at 2 in the afternoon.
I like seeing how the photos turned out.

I like to be helped through the holidays:
4th of July, Labor Day, Halloween, Thanksgiving,
Christmas, New Year's.

they know how to ride these rapids
and they are less afraid of love than I am.

they can make me laugh where professional comedians
fail.

there is walking out to buy a newspaper together.

there is much good in being alone
but there is a strange warmth in not being alone.

I like boiled red potatoes.
I like eyes and fingers better than mine that can
get knots out of shoelaces.

I like letting her drive the car on dark nights
when the road and the way have gotten to me,
the car radio on
we light cigarettes and talk about things
and now and then
become silent.

I like hairpins on tables.
I like knowing the same walls
the same people.

I dislike the insane and useless fights which always
occur
and I dislike myself at these times
giving nothing
understanding nothing.

I like boiled asparagus
I like radishes
green onions.
I like to put my car into a car wash.
I like it when I have ten win on a six to one
shot.
I like my radio which keeps playing
Shostakovich, Brahms, Beethoven, Mahler.

I like it when there's a knock on the door and
she's there.

no matter who I'm with
people always say,
are you still with her?

they must think I bury them in
the Hollywood Hills.

2nd. street, near Hollister, in Santa Monica

my daughter is 13 years old
and the other afternoon
I drove to her court to take her
to lunch
and there was a beautiful woman
sitting on the porch
and I thought, well, she'll get
up and tell Marina that
I'm here.
and the beautiful woman stood up
and walked toward me.
it was my daughter.
she said, "Hi!"
I answered as if everything were
commonplace and we drove off
together.

the trashing of the dildo

one week I had 6 different women
in 6 different beds
(I took a Thursday night off
to rest up)
and I only failed
sexually
one night,
the last night of the week:
it went down while I was in action.
she took it personally.

I am now down to one woman
and I don't cheat on her.
when you find you can get fucked
easily
you find you don't need to go
about
simply fucking women
and using their toilets and their
showers and their towels
and their insides,
their thoughts, their
feelings.

I now have a nice garden outside.
she planted it.
I water it daily.
potted plants hang from ropes.
I am at peace.
she stays 3 days a week
then goes back to her house.

the mailman asks me, "hey, what
happened to all your women? you
used to have a couple of them
sitting on your porch when I came
by . . ."

"Sam," I tell him, "I was beginning
to feel like a dildo . . ."

the liquor delivery man comes by:
"hey, man! where are all the *broads*?
you're alone tonight . . ."

"all the more to drink,
Ernie . . ."

I've done the town, I've drunk the
city, I've fucked the country, I've
pissed on the universe.
there's little left to do but
consolidate and ease out.

I have a nice garden.
I have a lovely woman.

I no longer feel like a
dildo.
I feel like a man.

it feels much
better, it
does. don't worry
about me.

a place to relax

to be a young fool and poor and ugly
doesn't make the walls look so good.
so many evenings, examining walls
with nothing to drink
nothing to smoke
nothing to eat
(we drank my paychecks fast).
she always knew when to leave.
she put me through her college—
she gave me my masters and my Ph.D.,
and she always came back,
she wanted a place to relax
somewhere to hang her clothes.
she claimed I was very funny,
I made her laugh
but I was not trying to be
funny.
she had beautiful legs and she was
intelligent but she just didn't care,
and all my fury and all my humor and
all my madness only entertained
her: I was performing for her
like some puppet in some hell of my own.
a few times when she left I had enough
cheap wine and enough cigarettes
to listen to the radio and look at the

walls and get drunk enough to get away
from her.
but she always came back to try me
again.
I do remember her especially.
other better women have made me feel as
bad
as those evenings
taking that two mile walk home from work
turning up the alley
looking up at the window
and finding the shades dark.
she taught me the agony of the damned and
the useless.
one wants good weather, good luck, good
dreams.
for me it was a long chance in a big field,
the time was cold and the longshot didn't
come in.
I buried her five years after I met her,
seldom seeing her in the last three.
there were only four at the grave:
the priest
her landlady
her son and myself.
it didn't matter:
all those walks up the alley
hoping for a light behind the shade.
all those dozens of men who had fucked her
were not there
and one of the men who had loved her
was: "My crazy stockroom boy from the
department store," she called me.

snap snap

oh, the ladies can get snappish
sticking their hands into the sink
yanking at sheets
working their trowels through the earth
near the radish patch
sitting in the auto with you
as you drive along.

oh, the ladies can get snappish
discussing
God and the movies
music and works of art
or what to do about the cat's
infection.
the snappishness spreads to
every area of conversation
the voice-pitch remains at
high-trill.

what happened to the nights
before the fire
when they were all sweetness
of ankle and knee

pure of eye
long hair combed out?

of course, we knew that wasn't
real
but the snappishness is.
love is too
but it's stuck somewhere
between the crab apple tree
and the sewer.

the judge is asleep in his
chambers and
nobody's guilty.

for the little one

she's downstairs singing, playing her
guitar, I think she's happier than
usual and I'm glad. sometimes my
mind gets sick and I'm cruel to her.
she weighs one hundred and one
pounds
has small wrists and
her eyes
are often purely sad.

sometimes my needs
make me selfish
a backwash takes my
mind
and I've never been
good
with apology.

I hear her singing
now it's
very late night
and from here
I can see the
lights of the city

and they are sweet as
ripe garden fruits
and this room is
calm
so strange
as if magic had
become normal.

hello, Barbara

25 years ago
in Las Vegas
I got married
the only time.

we were only
there an hour.
I drove all the
way up and all
the way back
to L.A.

and I still
didn't feel
married and
I continued
to feel that
way for 2 and
½ years until
she divorced
me.

then I found

a woman
who had ants
for pets and
fed them
sugar.
I got her
pregnant.

after that
there were
many other
women.
but the
other day
this man
who has been
looking into
my past
said, "I've
got the
phone number
of your
x-wife."

I put it
in my
dresser drawer.

then I got
drunk one
night

pulled the
number out
and
phoned her.

"hey, baby,
it's me!"

"I know it's
you," she said
in that same
chilly voice.

"how ya
doin'?"

"all right,"
she answered.

"you still
livin' on that
chicken ranch?"

"yes," she
said.

"well, I'm
drunk.
I just thought
I'd give you
a little
call."

"so you're
drunk again,"
she said in
that same
chilly voice.

"yes. well,
all right,
I'm saying
goodbye now . . ."

"goodbye," she
said and hung
up.

I walked over
and poured a
new drink.
after 25 years
she still
hated me.

I didn't think
I was that
bad.

of course,
guys like me
seldom
do.

Carson McCullers

she died of alcoholism
wrapped in the blanket
of a deck chair
on an overseas
steamer

all her books of
terrified loneliness

all her books about
the cruelty
of the loveless lover

were all that were left
of her

as the strolling vacationer
discovered her body

notified the captain

and she was dispatched
somewhere else
upon the ship

as everything else
continued
as
she had written it.

Jane and Droll

we were in a small shack in
central L.A.

there was a woman in bed
with me

and there was a very large
dog
at the foot of the bed

and as they slept
I listened to them
breathe

and I thought, they depend
upon me.
how very curious.

I still had that thought
in the morning
after our breakfast
while backing the car
out of the drive

the woman and the dog
on the front step
sitting and watching
me

as I laughed and waved
and as she smiled and
waved

and the dog looked
as I backed into the
street and disappeared
into the city.

now tonight
I still think of them
sitting on that
front step

it's like an old
movie—35 years
old—that nobody ever
saw or understood
but me

and even though the
critics would dub it
ordinary

I like it
very much.

we get along

the various women I have lived with have attended
rock concerts, reggae festivals, love-ins, peace
marches, movies, garage sales, fairs, protests,
weddings, funerals, poetry readings, Spanish classes,
spas, parties, bars and so forth
and I have lived with this
machine.

while the ladies attended affairs, saved the whales,
the seals, the dolphins, the great white shark,
while the ladies talked on the telephone
this machine and I lived
together.

as we live together tonight: this machine, the 3
cats, the radio and the wine.

after I die the ladies will say (if asked): "he
liked to sleep, to drink; he never wanted to go
anywhere . . . well, the racetrack, *that* stupid
place!"

the ladies I have known and lived with have been
very social, jumping into the car, waving, going
out there as if some treasure of great import
awaited them . . .

"it's a new punk group, they're great!"
"Allen Ginsberg's reading!"
"I'm late for my dance class!"
"I'm going to play scrabble with Rita!"
"it's a surprise birthday for Fran!"

I have this machine.
this machine and I live together.

Olympia, that's her name.
a good girl.

almost always
faithful.

it was all right

she's a good old girl now.
she's fattened and grayed.

we were lovers many years
ago,
there was a child,
there is a child,
now a woman.

this woman gave me
a tape
of her mother
talking about poetry
and her life and
reading her
poems.

an hour-long tape.

I listened to it.
unfortunately
the poetry wasn't
very good
but most poetry
isn't.

she went on talking
about
poetry workshops,
various influences—
family, friends, her
husband (I
wasn't) who didn't
seem to like her
writing poetry.

she kept a notebook
near her bed
and one in her
purse.

she talked about
this and that.

I was happy for her
that they allowed her
on a radio station
for an hour.
I'd heard worse
from professors who
had made
literature
their trade.

and as I listened
to her voice
it was the
same voice

I'd heard
20 years ago

when I dropped in
on her place
on Vermont Avenue
and found her
feeding sugar
to the ants
in her room
and there were
many ants
there
but she had
a great body
then
and I was
hard-up as
hell.

it was a
good hour,
Fran.

my walls of love

it's on nights like this, I get back what I
can.
the living is hard, the writing is free.

were that the women were as easy
but they wore always much the same:
they liked my writing in finished book-
form
but there was always something about the
actual *typing*
working toward the new
which bothered them . . .

I wasn't competing with them
but they got competitive with me
in forms and styles which I didn't consider
either original or creative
although to me
they were certainly
astonishing enough.

now they are set loose
with themselves and the others

and have new problems
in another way.

all those lovelies:
I'm glad I'm with them in spirit
rather than in the flesh

as now I can bang this fucking machine
without concern.

eulogy to a hell of a dame

some dogs who sleep at night
must dream of bones
and I remember your bones
in flesh
and best
in that dark green dress
and those high-heeled bright
black shoes,
you always cursed when you
drank,
your hair coming down, you
wanted to explode out of
what was holding you:
rotten memories of a
rotten
past, and
you finally got
out
by dying,
leaving me with the
rotten
present;
you've been dead
28 years
yet I remember you

better than any of
them;
you were the only one
who understood
the futility of the
arrangement of
life;
all the others were
displeased with
trivial segments,
carped
nonsensically about
nonsense;
Jane, you were
killed by
knowing too much.
here's a drink
to your bones
that
this dog
still
dreams about.

love

I've seen old pairs
sitting in rockers
across from each other
being congratulated and celebrated
for being together 50 or 60
years
who would have
so long ago
settled for anything
else
but fate
fear and
circumstance
bound them,
and as we tell them
how wonderful they are
in their great and enduring
love
only they
really know
but can't tell us
that from their first
meeting
on

it didn't mean
all that
like
waiting on death
now.
it's about the
same.

eulogy

with old cars, especially when you buy them second
hand and drive them for many years,
a love affair begins:
you have memorized each wire on the engine
the dash and elsewhere,
you are overly familiar with the
carburetor
the plugs
the throttle arm
other sundry
parts.
you have learned all the tricks to
. keep the affair going,
you even know how to slam the glove compartment so that
it will stay closed,
how to slap the headlights with an open palm
in order to have
light,
and you know how many times to pump the gas
and how long to wait
to start the motor,
and you know each hole in the
upholstery
and the shape of each spring

sticking through;
the car has been in and out of
police impounds,
has been ticketed for various
malfunctions:
broken wipers in the rain,
no turn signals at night, no
brake lights, broken tail lights, bad
brakes, excessive
exhaust and so on . . .
but for it all
you knew it so well
there was never an accident, the
old car moved you from one place to
another,
almost faithfully
—the poor man's miracle.
and when that *last* breakdown arrives,
when the valves quit,
when the tired piston arms weary and
break, or the
crankshaft falls out and
you must sell it for
junk
—to watch it carted
away
hung there
wheeled off
as if it had no
soul, no
meaning,

the thin rear tires
and the back windshield
the twisted license plate
are the last things you
see, and it
hurts
as if some human you loved very
much
and lived with
day after day
had died
and you are the only
one
to have known
the music
the magic
the unbelievable
gallantry.

40 years ago in that hotel room

off of Union Avenue, 3 a.m., Jane and I had been
drinking cheap wine since noon and I walked barefoot
across the rugs, picking up shards of broken glass
(in the daylight you could see them under the skin,
blue lumps working toward the heart) and I walked in
my torn shorts, ugly balls hanging out, my twisted and
torn undershirt spotted with cigarette holes of various
sizes. I stopped before Jane who sat in her drunken
chair.
then I screamed at her:
"I'M A GENIUS AND NOBODY KNOWS IT BUT
ME!"

she shook her head, sneered and slurred through her
lips:
"shit! you're a fucking
asshole!"

I stalked across the floor, this time picking up a
piece of glass much larger than usual, and I reached down
and plucked it out: a lovely large speared chunk dripping
with my blood, I flung it off into space, turned and glared
at Jane:

"you don't know anything, you
whore!"

"FUCK YOU!" she
screamed.

then the phone rang and I picked it up and
yelled: "I'M A GENIUS AND NOBODY KNOWS IT BUT
ME!"

it was the desk clerk: "Mr. Chinaski, I've warned you
again and again, you are keeping all our
guests awake . . ."

"GUESTS?" I laughed, "YOU MEAN THOSE FUCKING
WINOS?"

then Jane was there and she grabbed the phone and
yelled: "I'M A FUCKING GENIUS TOO AND I'M THE
ONLY WHORE WHO KNOWS IT!"

and she hung up.

then I walked over and put the
chain on the door.
then Jane and I pushed the sofa in
front of the door
turned out the lights
and sat up in bed
waiting for them,
we were well aware of the

location of the drunk
tank: North Avenue
21—such a fancy sounding
address.

we each had a chair at the
side of the bed,
and each chair held ashtray,
cigarettes and
wine.

they came with much
sound:
"is this the right
door?"
"yeah," he said,
"413."

one of them beat with
the end of his night
stick:
"L.A. POLICE DEPARTMENT!
OPEN UP IN THERE!"

we did not
open up in there.

then they both beat with
their night sticks:
"OPEN UP! OPEN UP IN
THERE!"

now all the guests were
awake for sure.

"come on, open up," one of them
said more quietly, "we just want to
talk a bit, nothing more . . ."

"nothing more," said the other
one, "we might even have a little drink
with you . . ."

30–40 years ago
North Avenue 21 was a terrible place,
40 or 50 men slept on the same floor
and there was one toilet which nobody dared
excrete upon.

"we know that you're nice people, we just
want to meet you . . ."
one of them said.

"yeah," the other one said.

then we heard them
whispering.
we didn't hear them walk
away.
we were not sure that they
were gone.

"holy shit," Jane asked,
"do you think they're
gone?"

"shhhh . . ."
I hissed.

we sat there in the dark
sipping at our
wine.
there was nothing to do
but watch two neon signs
through the window to the
east
one was near the library
and said
in red:
JESUS SAVES.
the other sign was more
interesting:
it was a large red bird
which flapped its wings
seven times
and then a sign lit up
below it
advertising
SIGNAL GASOLINE.

it was as good a life
as we could
afford.

a magician, gone

they go one by one and as they do it gets closer
to me and
I don't mind that so much, it's
just that I can't be practical about the
mathematics that take others
to the vanishing point.

last Saturday
one of racing's greatest harness drivers
died—little Joe O'Brien.
I had seen him win many a
race. he
had a peculiar rocking motion
he flicked the reins
and rocked his body back and
forth. he
applied this motion
during the stretch run and
it was quite dramatic and
effective . . .

he was so small that he couldn't
lay the whip on as hard as the
others

so
he rocked and rocked
in the sulky
and the horse felt the lightning
of his excitement
that rhythmic crazy rocking was
transferred from man to
beast . . .
the whole thing had the feel of a
crapshooter calling to the
gods, and the gods
so often answered . . .

I saw Joe O'Brien win
endless photo finishes
many by a
nose.
he'd take a horse
another driver couldn't get a
run out of
and Joe would put his touch
to it
and the animal would
most often respond with
a flurry of wild energy.
Joe O'Brien was the finest harness driver
I had ever seen
and I'd seen many over the
decades.
nobody could nurse and cajole
a trotter or a pacer

like little Joe
nobody could make the magic work
like Joe.

they go one by one
presidents
garbage men
killers
actors
pickpockets
boxers
hit men
ballet dancers
fishermen
doctors
fry cooks
like
that

but Joe O'Brien
it's going to be hard
hard
to find a replacement for
little Joe

and
at the ceremony
held for him
at the track tonight
(Los Alamitos 10-1-84)
as the drivers gathered in a

circle
in their silks
at the finish line
I had to turn my back
to the crowd
and climb the upper grandstand
steps
to the wall
so the people wouldn't
see me
cry.

no luck for that

there is a place in the heart that
will never be filled

a space

and even during the
best moments
and
the greatest of
times

we will know it

we will know it
more than
ever

there is a place in the heart that
will never be filled

and

we will wait
and
wait

in that
space.

love poem to a stripper

50 years ago I watched the girls
shake it and strip
at The Burbank and The Follies
and it was very sad
and very dramatic
as the light turned from green to
purple to pink
and the music was loud and
vibrant,
now I sit here tonight
smoking and drinking
listening to classical
music
but I still remember some of
their names: Darlene, Candy, Jeanette
and Rosalie.
-Rosalie was the
best, she knew how,
and we twisted in our seats and
made sounds
as Rosalie brought magic
to the lonely
so long ago.

now Rosalie
either so very old or

so quiet under the
earth,
this is the pimple-faced
kid
who lied about his
age
just to watch
you.

you were good, Rosalie
in 1935,
good enough to remember
now
when the light is
yellow
and the nights are
slow.

BUK

love crushed like a dead fly

in many ways
I had come upon lucky times
but was still living in this
bomb-struck court off the
avenue.

I had battered my way through
many layers of
adversity:

being an uneducated man
with
wild mad dreams—
some of them had
evolved (I mean, if
you're going to be here
you might as well fight
for the miracle).

but
at once
as such things occur—
the lady I loved
let off

and began to
fuck
around the block
with
strangers
imbeciles
and probably some fairly good
sorts

but
as such things occur—
it was without
warning
and along with it
the pitiable dull languor of
disbelief
and
that painful mindless
clawing.

and also
in the turning of the
tides
I broke out
with a huge boil
near
apple-size, well, half a
small apple
but still a
monstrosity of
horror.

I pulled the phone
from the wall
locked the door
pulled the shades and
drank
just to pass the time of
day and night, went
mad, probably,
but
in a strange and
delicious
sense.

found an old record
played it
over and over—
a certain roaring section of
the tonality
fitting exactly into my
cage
my place
my
disenchantment—
love dead like a crushed
fly,
I was reaching back and
wandering through my
idiocy, realizing that as a
being
I could have been
better—

not to her
but to
the grocery clerk
the corner paperboy
the stray cat
the bartender
and/or
etc.

we keep coming up
short and
shorter
but
ultimately
are not so terrible
as all that, then
get a girlfriend who
fucks
around the block
and
a boil near apple-
size.

remembering then
the chances
turned away,
some from lovely
ones (at that
moment)
not many
but some

fucks
turned away
in honor of
her.

ah, redemption and
remorse!

and the bottle
and the record
playing over and
over—

asshole, asshole, ass-
hole, be hard like the
world,
gear up for
disintegration—

what a record it was
as you stumbled over the beer and
whiskey bottles
the shorts
the shirts
the memories
besotted across the
room.

you came out of it
two weeks later
to find her

in your doorway
on a 9 a.m.
morning

hair neatly
done,
smiling
as if all occurrence
had been
blotted out.

she was just a
dumb
game-playing
bitch

having tried the
others and
finding them (in
one way or the
other)
insufficient

she was
back (she
thought)
as you poured her a
beer and
tilted the Scotch
into your early
glass

remembering
exactly and forever
the sounds of that record
heard again and
again:

the gift of her had
ended, new
failures were about to
begin

as she crossed her long
legs
made that smile
smile
and said,
gaily, "well, what have you
been
doing?"

shoes

when you're young
a pair of
female
high-heeled shoes
just sitting
alone
in the closet
can fire your
bones;
when you're old
it's just
a pair of shoes
without
anybody
in them
and
just as
well.

pulled down shade

what I like about you
she told me
is that you're crude—
look at you sitting there
a beercan in your hand
and a cigar in your mouth
and look at
your dirty hairy belly
sticking out from
under your shirt.
you've got your shoes off
and you've got a hole
in your right stocking
with the big toe
sticking out.
you haven't shaved in
4 or 5 days.
your teeth are yellow
and your eyebrows
hang down
all twisted
and you've got enough
scars
to scare the shit
out of anybody.

there's always
a ring
in your bathtub
your telephone
is covered with
grease
and
half the crap in
your refrigerator is
rotten.
you never
wash your car.
you've got newspapers
a week old
on the floor.
you read dirty
magazines
and you don't have
a tv
but you order
deliveries from the
liquor store
and you tip
good.
and best of all
you don't push
a woman to
go to bed
with you.
you seem hardly
interested
and when I talk to you

you don't
say anything
you just
look around
the room or
scratch your
neck
like you don't
hear me.
you've got an old
wet towel in
the sink
and a photo of
Mussolini
on the wall
and you never
complain
about anything
and you never
ask questions
and I've
known you for
6 months
but I have
no idea
who you are.
you're like
some
pulled down shade
but that's what
I like about
you:

your crudeness:
a woman can
drop
out of your
life and
forget you
real fast.
a woman
can't go anywhere
but UP
after
leaving you,
honey.
you've got to
be
the best thing
that ever
happened
to
a girl
who's between
one guy
and the next
and has nothing
to do
at the moment.
this fucking
Scotch is
great.
let's play
Scrabble.

Trollius and trellises

of course, I may die in the next ten minutes
and I'm ready for that
but what I'm really worried about is
that my editor-publisher might retire
even though he is ten years younger than
I.
it was just 25 years ago (I was at that *ripe*
old age of 45)
when we began our unholy alliance to
test the literary waters,
neither of us being much
known.

I think we had some luck and still have some
of same
yet
the odds are pretty fair
that he will opt for warm and pleasant
afternoons
in the garden
long before I.

writing is its own intoxication
while publishing and editing,

attempting to collect bills
carries its own
attrition
which also includes dealing with the
petty bitchings and demands
of many
so-called genius darlings who are
not.

I won't blame him for getting
out
and hope he sends me photos of his
Rose Lane, his
Gardenia Avenue.

will I have to seek other
promulgators?
that fellow in the Russian
fur hat?
or that beast in the East
with all that hair
in his ears, with those wet and
greasy lips?

or will my editor-publisher
upon exiting for that world of Trollius and
trellis
hand over the
machinery
of his former trade to a
cousin, a

daughter or
some Poundian from Big
Sur?
or will he just pass the legacy on
to the
Shipping Clerk
who will rise like
Lazarus,
fingering new-found
importance?

one can imagine terrible
things:
"Mr. Chinaski, all your work
must now be submitted in
Rondo form
and
typed
triple-spaced on rice
paper."

power corrupts,
life aborts
and all you
have left
is a
bunch of
warts.

"no, no, Mr. Chinaski:
Rondo form!"

"hey, man," I'll ask,
"haven't you heard of
the thirties?"

"the thirties? what's
that?"

my present editor-publisher
and I
at times
did discuss the thirties,
the Depression
and
some of the little tricks it
taught us—
like how to endure on almost
nothing
and move forward
anyhow.

well, John, if it happens enjoy your
divertissement to
plant husbandry,
cultivate and aerate
between
bushes, water only in the
early morning, spread
shredding to discourage
weed growth
and
as I do in my writing:
use plenty of
manure.

and thank you
for locating me there at
5124 DeLongpre Avenue
somewhere between
alcoholism and
madness.

together we
laid down the gauntlet
and there are takers
even at this late date
still to be
found
as the fire sings
through the
trees.

turn

I learned recently
that my first wife
died in
India.

she belonged to some
cult and died of a
mysterious
disease.

the family didn't
ask
to have the body
shipped
back.

poor Barbara,
she was born with a
neck
that couldn't
turn.

a beautiful woman
otherwise.

my dear, high in the
sun, I hope that your
neck
turns
at last

and that the stares
and the ridicule
and the unwanted
pity

find home
elsewhere.

oh, I was a ladies' man!

you
wonder about
when
you ran through women
like an open-field
maniac
with this total
disregard for
panties, dishtowels,
photos
and all the other
accoutrements—
like
the tangling of
souls.

what
were you
trying to
do
trying to
catch up
with?

it was like a
hunt.

how many
could you
bag?
move
onto?

names
shoes
dresses
sheets, bathrooms,
bedrooms, kitchens
front
rooms,
cafes,
pets,
names of pets,
names of children;
middle names, last
names, made-up
names.

you proved it was
easy.
you proved it
could be done
again and
again,
those legs held
high
behind most of
you.
or

they were on top
or
you were
behind
or
both
sideways
plus
other
inventions.

songs on radios.
parked cars.
telephone voices.
the pouring of
drinks.
the senseless
conversations.

now you know
you were nothing but a
fucking
dog, or
a snail wrapped around
a snail—
sticky shells in the
sunlight, or in
the misty evenings,
or in the dark
dark.

you were
nature's
idiot,
not proving but
being
proved.
not a man but a
plan
unfolding,
not thrusting but
being
thrust.
now
you know.

then
you thought you were
such a
clever devil
such a
cad
such a
man-bull
such a
bad boy

smiling over your
wine
planning your next
move

what a
waste of time
you were

you great
rider
you Attila of
the springs and
elsewhere

you could have
slept through it
all
and you would never
have been
missed

never would have
been
missed
at
all.

love poem

half-past nowhere
in the crumbling
tower
let the worms seize
glory

dark inside of
darkness

the last gamble
lost

reaching
for

bone
silence.

a dog

look at you, stockings and shorts, beer cans
on the floor, you don't want to communicate,
to you a woman is nothing but something
for your convenience, you just sit there
slurping it up, why don't you say something?

this is your place so you can't leave, if I were
talking like this at my place you'd walk right
out the door.

why are you smiling?
is something funny?

all you do is slurp it up and go to the racetrack!
what's so great about a horse?
what's a horse got that I haven't got?

four legs?

aren't you bright?
now aren't you the thing?

you act like nothing matters!
well, let me tell you, asshole, I matter!
you think you're the only man in this town?

well, let me tell you, there are plenty of men who
want me, my body, my mind, my spirit!

people have asked me, "What are you doing
with a person like that?"

what?
no, I don't want a drink!
I want you to realize what's happening before
it's too late!

look at you still slurping it down!
you know what happens to you when you drink
too much!
I might as well be living with a eunuch!

my mother warned me!
everybody warned me!

look at you now!
why don't you shave?
you've spilled wine all over your shirt!
and that cheap cigar!
you know what that thing smells
like?
horseshit!

hey, where you going?
some bar, some stinking bar!
you'll sit there nursing your self-pity
with all those other losers!

if you go through that door I'm going
out dancing!
I'm going to have some fun!

if you go out that door, then that's
it!

all right, go on then, you asshole!

asshole!

asshole!

ASSHOLE!

the strong man

I went to see him, there in that place in
Echo Park
after my shift at the
post office.
he was a huge bearded fellow
and he sat in his chair like a
Buddha
and he was my Buddha, my guru
my hero, my roar of
light.
sometimes he wasn't kind
but he was always quite more than
interesting.
to come from the post office
slaves
to that explosion of light
confounded me,
but it was a remarkable and
delightful
confusion.

thousands of books upon
hundreds of subjects
lay rotting in his
cellar.

to play chess with him was
to be laughed off the
boards.
to challenge him
physically or
mentally was
useless.

but he had the ability to
listen to your
persiflage
patiently
and then the ability
to sum up its
weaknesses,
its delusions in
one sentence.

I often wondered how
he put up with my
railings; he was kind,
after all.

the nights lasted 7,
8 hours.
I had my libations.
he had himself,
and a beautiful woman
who quietly smiled as she
listened to
us.

she worked at a drawing
board,
designing things.
I never asked what and
she never
said.

the walls and the ceilings
were pasted over
with hundreds of odd
sayings—
like the last words of
a man in an electric
chair,
or gangsters on their
death beds,
of an old moll's instructions
to her children;
photos of Hitler, Al Capone,
Chief Sitting Bull,
Lucky Luciano.
it was an endless honey-
comb of strange faces
and
utterances.

it was darkly refreshing.

and at odd rare times
even I got good.

then the Buddha would
nod.

he had everything on
tape.

sometimes on another
night he would play a
tape back for
me.
and then I would
realize how pitiful, how
cheap, how
inept I sounded.

he seldom missed.

at times I wondered why
the world had not
discovered
him.
he made no effort to be
discovered.
he had other
visitors,
always wild, original
refreshing
folk.

it was crazier than the
sun burning up the
sea,
it was the bats of hell
whirling about the
room.
it was the clearance
of crap from the
slashed
psyche.

night after night after
night, I
filled, I flew, I was doused
in a special
wonderment.

that was decades ago
and he is still
alive, and
I.

he made a place when
there was no
place.
a place to go when all
was closing in,
strangling, crushing,
debilitating,
when there was no
voice, no sound,

no sense,
he lent the easy
saving
natural
grace.

I feel that I owe him
one,
I feel that I owe him
many.

but I can hear him
now, that same
voice
as when he sat
so huge
in that same
chair:

"Nothing is owed,
Bukowski."

you're finally wrong,
this time,
John Thomas, you
bastard.

the bluebird

there's a bluebird in my heart that
wants to get out
but I'm too tough for him,
I say, stay in there, I'm not going
to let anybody see
you.

there's a bluebird in my heart that
wants to get out
but I pour whiskey on him and inhale
cigarette smoke
and the whores and the bartenders
and the grocery clerks
never know that
he's
in there.

there's a bluebird in my heart that
wants to get out
but I'm too tough for him,
I say,
stay down, do you want to mess
me up?
you want to screw up the

works?
you want to blow my book sales in
Europe?

there's a bluebird in my heart that
wants to get out
but I'm too clever, I only let him out
at night sometimes
when everybody's asleep.
I say, I know that you're there,
so don't be
sad.

then I put him back,
but he's singing a little
in there, I haven't quite let him
die
and we sleep together like
that
with our
secret pact
and it's nice enough to
make a man
weep, but I don't
weep, do
you?

the dressmaker

my first wife made her own dresses,
which I thought was nice.
I'd often see her sitting over her
sewing machine
putting together a new dress.
we were both working and I thought
it was great that she found the time
to put together her
wardrobe.

then one evening I came home and
she was crying.
she told me that some guy at work
had told her that she had bad
taste in her wearing
apparel,
 said she looked
"tacky."

"do you think I dress tacky?"
 she asked.
"of course not.
 who is this guy?
 I'll beat hell out of him!"

"you can't, he's a homosexual."

"god damn it!"

she cried some more that
evening.
I tried to reassure her and she
finally stopped.

but after that, she purchased
her dresses.
they didn't look nearly as well
but she told me that the fellow
had praised her on her new
taste.

well, as long as she stopped
crying.

then one day she asked me, "which do
you like me best in, the old dresses or
the new ones?"

"you look good either way,"
I answered.

"no, but which do you prefer?
the old dresses or the new ones?"

"the old ones," I told her.

then she began crying again.

there were similar problems with other
parts of our
marriage.

when she divorced me she was still
wearing store-purchased
dresses.

but she took the sewing machine
with her
and a suitcase full of the old
dresses.

confessions

waiting for death
like a cat
that will jump on the
bed

I am so very sorry for
my wife

she will see this
stiff
white
body

shake it once, then
maybe
again:

"Hank!"

Hank won't
answer.

it's not my death that
worries me, it's my wife
left with this

pile of
nothing.

I want to
let her know
though
that all the nights
sleeping
beside her
even the useless
arguments
were things
ever splendid

and the hard
words
I ever feared to
say
can now be
said:

I love
you.

Sources

As in *On Cats* (Ecco, 2015), all the poems in *On Love* are faithful reproductions of the manuscripts Bukowski submitted to small press editors; editorial changes have been kept to a minimum. If a given manuscript could not be found, then the appropriate magazine version was used in an attempt to preserve Bukowski's voice and style—the poems published by Black Sparrow Press, especially in the case of the posthumous collections, were dramatically changed. The sources below indicate which version is being used for each poem as well as its date of publication.

"mine." *Semina* 2, December 1957; collected in *The Days Run Like Wild Horses Over the Hills*, 1969.

"layover." *The Naked Ear* 9, late 1957; collected in *The Roominghouse Madrigals*, 1988.

"the day I kicked a bankroll out the window." *Quicksilver* 12.2, Summer 1959; collected in *The Roominghouse* . . .

"I taste the ashes of your death." *Nomad* 1, Winter 1959; collected in *The Days* . . .

"love is a piece of paper torn to bits." *Coastlines* 14-15, Spring 1960; collected in *The Roominghouse* . . .

"to the whore who took my poems." *Quagga* 1.3, September 1960; collected in *Burning in Water, Drowning in Fire*, 1974.

"shoes." Late 1960 manuscript; collected in *The People Look Like Flowers at Last*, 2007.

"a real thing, a good woman." Early 1961 manuscript; collected in *Come On In!*, 2006.

"one night stand." Late 1961 manuscript; collected in *The Rooming-house* . . .

"the mischief of expiration." February 1962 manuscript; collected as "beauty gone" in *Open All Night*, 2000.

"love is a form of selfishness." *Mummy*, 1962; previously uncollected.

"for Jane: with all the love I had, which was not enough." 1962 manuscript; collected in *The Days* . . .

"for Jane." *The Wormwood Review* 8, December 1962; collected in *The Days* . . .

"notice." *Sciamachy* 5, 1963; collected in *The Days* . . .

"my real love in Athens." *Nadada* 1, August 1964; previously uncollected.

"sleeping woman." *The Wormwood Review* 16, December 1964; collected in *The Days* . . .

"a party here—machineguns, tanks, an army fighting against men on rooftops." *Kauri* 10, October 1965; previously uncollected.

"for the 18 months of Marina Louise." 1965 manuscript; collected as "Marina" in *Mockingbird Wish Me Luck*, 1972.

"poem for my daughter." *Showcase* 3, July 1966; collected in *The People Look Like* . . .

"answer to a note found in the mailbox." *Salted Feathers* 10, August 1967; previously uncollected.

"all the love of me goes out to her (for A.M.)." Late 1969 manuscript, first titled "the waitress"; previously uncollected.

"an answer to a critic of sorts." *Stooge* 5, 1970; previously uncollected.

"the shower." March 1971 manuscript; collected in *Mockingbird* . . .

"2 carnations." April 26, 1971 manuscript; collected in *Mockingbird* . . .

"have you ever kissed a panther?" May 1971 manuscript; collected in *Mockingbird* . . .

"the best love poem I can write at the moment." June 15, 1971 manuscript; previously uncollected.

"balling." November 2, 1971 manuscript; previously uncollected.

"hot." *Event* 2.2, 1972; collected in *Burning* . . .

"smiling, shining, singing." December 22, 1972 manuscript; collected in *What Matters Most Is How Well You Walk Through the Fire*, 1999.

"visit to Venice." *Vagabond* 17, 1973; previously uncollected.

"love poem to Marina." *Second Coming* 2.3, 1973; previously uncollected.

"I can hear the sound of human lives being ripped to pieces." c. 1973 manuscript; collected as "the sound of human lives" in *Burning* . . .

"for those 3." Early 1970s manuscript; previously unpublished.

"blue moon, oh bleweeww mooooon how I adore you!". June 27, 1974 manuscript; collected in *Play the Piano Drunk Like a Percussion Instrument Until the Fingers Begin to Bleed a Bit*, 1979. This poem is part of a longer poem, "extant," which remains uncollected.

"the first love." July 21, 1974 manuscript; collected as "first love" in *Bone Palace Ballet*, 1997.

"love." August 2, 1974 manuscript; collected as "sloppy love" in *What Matters* . . .

"raw with love (for N.W.)." *Los Angeles Free Press* 530, September 1974; collected in *What Matters* . . .

"a love poem for all the women I have known." September 15, 1974 manuscript (second draft); collected as "a love poem" in *War All The Time*, 1984.

"fax." January 23, 1975 manuscript (second draft); collected as "sweet music" in *Love Is a Dog from Hell*, 1977, and as "it beats love" in *The Night Torn Mad with Footsteps*, 2001.

"one for the shoeshine man." May 17, 1975 manuscript; collected in *Love Is a Dog* . . .

"who in the hell is Tom Jones?". June 4, 1975 manuscript; collected in *Love Is a Dog* . . .

"sitting in a sandwich joint just off the freeway." June 22, 1975 manuscript; collected as "sitting in a sandwich joint" in *Love Is a Dog* . . .

"a definition." November 15, 1975 manuscript; collected in *The Night Torn* . . .

"an acceptance slip." November 27, 1975 manuscript; collected in *Love Is a Dog* . . . as "my old man," and as "acceptance" in *The People Look Like* . . .

"the end of a short affair." January 19, 1976 manuscript; collected in *Love Is a Dog* . . .

"one for old snaggle-tooth." January 23, 1976 manuscript; collected in *Love Is a Dog* . . .

"prayer for a whore in bad weather." February 7, 1976 manuscript; collected as "prayer in bad weather" in *Love Is a Dog* . . .

"I made a mistake." *Scarlet*, April 1976; collected in *Love Is a Dog* . . .

"the 6 foot goddess (for S.D.)." June 4, 1976 manuscript; collected in *Love Is a Dog* . . .

"quiet clean girls in gingham dresses." September 15, 1976 manuscript; collected in *Love Is a Dog* . . .

"tonight." September 23, 1976 manuscript; collected in *Love Is a Dog* . . .

"pacific telephone." November 1, 1976 manuscript; collected in *Love Is a Dog* . . .

"hunchback." November 20, 1976 manuscript; collected in *What Matters* . . .

"mermaid." October 9, 1977 manuscript; collected in *Play the Piano* . . .

"yes." November 9, 1977 manuscript; collected in *Dangling in the Tournefortia*, 1981.

"2nd. street, near Hollister, in Santa Monica." December 18, 1977 manuscript; previously uncollected.

"the trashing of the dildo." June 30, 1978 manuscript; previously uncollected.

"a place to relax." May 21, 1979 manuscript; collected in *What Matters* . . .

"snap snap." June 28, 1979 manuscript; collected in *Dangling* . . .

"for the little one." July 19, 1980 manuscript; collected in *Dangling* . . .

"hello, Barbara." January 2, 1981 manuscript; collected in *Dangling* . . . An early, shorter draft of this poem, "upon phoning an x-wife not seen for 20 years," dated October 19, 1977, appeared in *Open All Night*.

"Carson McCullers." October 24, 1981 manuscript; collected in *The Night Torn* . . .

"Jane and Droll." December 13, 1981 manuscript; collected as "Jane and Prince" in *Open All Night*.

"we get along." June 11, 1982 manuscript; collected in *Open All Night*.

"it was all right." June 22, 1982 manuscript; previously unpublished.

"my walls of love." February 20, 1983 manuscript; previously unpublished.

"eulogy to a hell of a dame." June 12, 1983 manuscript; collected in *War All the Time*.

"love." January 7, 1984 manuscript; collected as "endless love" in *Come On In!*

"eulogy." January 24, 1984 manuscript; collected in *The Night Torn* . . .

"40 years ago in that hotel room." February 1984 manuscript; collected in *The Night Torn* . . .

"a magician, gone." October 8, 1984 manuscript (second draft); collected in *You Get So Alone at Times That It Just Makes Sense*, 1986.

"no luck for that." January 21, 1985 manuscript; collected as "no help for that" in *You Get So Alone* . . .

"love poem to a stripper." February 1985 manuscript; collected in *You Get So Alone* . . .

"love crushed like a dead fly." October 1985 manuscript; collected as "love dead like a crushed fly" in *The Night Torn* . . .

"shoes." Late 1985 manuscript; collected in *You Get So Alone* . . .

"pulled down shade." October 1986 manuscript; collected in *The Last Night of Earth Poems*, 1992.

"Trollius and trellises." *Long Shot* 7, 1988; collected in *The Last Night* . . .

"turn." c. 1989 manuscript; previously unpublished.

"oh, I was a ladies' man!". c. 1989 manuscript; collected in *The Last Night* . . .

"love poem." January 7, 1990 manuscript; collected as "cancer" in *Come On In!*

"a dog." *Gas* 2, 1991; collected as "this dog" in *Sifting Through the Madness for the Word, the Line, the Way*, 2003.

"the strong man." March 29, 1991 manuscript; collected in *Betting on the Muse*, 1996.

"the bluebird." *the bluebird* broadside, September 1991; collected in *The Last Night* . . .

"the dressmaker." *Whoreson Dog* 1, 1993; collected in *Sifting* . . .

"confessions." *Red Cedar Review* 4, 1993; collected as "confession" in *The Last Night* . . .

Acknowledgments

The editor and publisher would like to thank the owners of the material here printed, which include the following institutions:

> University of Arizona, Special Collections Center
> The University of California, Santa Barbara, Special
>   Collections
> The Huntington Library, San Marino, California
> The State University of New York at Buffalo, Poetry/Rare
>   Book Collection
> The University of Southern California, USC Libraries,
>   Special Collections
> Temple University, Special Collections

Thanks also to the following periodicals, where some of the poems were first printed: *Coastlines*, *Event*, *Gas*, *Kauri*, *Long Shot*, *Los Angeles Free Press*, *Mummy*, *Nadada*, *The Naked Ear*, *Nomad*, *Quagga*, *Quicksilver*, *Red Cedar Review*, *Salted Feathers*, *Sciamachy*, *Second Coming*, *Semina*, *Showcase*, *Stooge*, *Vagabond*, *Whoreson Dog*, and *Wormwood Review*.